Big Ideas, Small Farm:
A marketing guide for attracting customers, increasing profitability, and building community.

A Grow Your Own Way Publication

Printed in the United States of America

First Printing, 2019

ISBN 0-9000000-0-0

Grow Your Own Farm Educational Services
1278 Mill Creek Circle
Salem, AR 72576
www.GrowYourOwnWayPublishing.com
www.GrowYourOwnSeminars.com

"Let us not forget that the cultivation of the Earth is the most important labor of man. When tillage begins, other arts will follow. The farmers, therefore, are the founders of civilization."
~ **Daniel Webster**

About this book

This book is different. The first part of this book reads like a self-help book, while the second part reads like a marketing book. This is by design because marketing tips, strategies, and theories are most effective when the person implementing them believes in them.

Marketing is a mindset as much as it is a practice. This mindset requires believing big ideas create big results. Effective marketing will turn your small farm into a sustainable business that will become your life's legacy.

Small farms are declining. This is not new; there are several reasons for this decline with plenty of blame to go around. Reciting those reasons will not reverse that trend; placing blame on other people, groups, or organizations is not going to grow your farm.

There are successful small farms. Your farm can become a successful business. The key is developing an effective business strategy that focuses on quality products, customer experience, and creating value for its customers.

This book is for the people who want to grow their small farm. This book includes 39 broad strategies broken down into 376 best practices designed to transform your small farm from a hobby into a substantial business.

Becoming the Big Idea

*"Ideas come from everything" ~ **Alfred Hitchcock***

Big success comes from big ideas. Big ideas transform small farms into viable businesses allowing owners to support families, create value for customers, and to live their farm dreams.

Big ideas illuminate the future. Approaching a small farm with hard work and vision provides a firm foundation for success. In today's world, small farms compete with mega-corporations, who employ thousands of people whose jobs are to destroy the competition. You are part of the competition!

This is a modern-day David and Goliath story; being a small farmer puts you in an epic battle whether you want to be or not. In addition to the corporate competition, there are legal issues and regulations, various barriers to entry for many markets, multiple activists who are going to accuse you of wronging someone or something somewhere, as well as an endless supply of other problems, issues, and setbacks.

Vision shows a pathway around these obstacles. These obstacles highlight opportunities. Many small farmers interpret these obstacles as a reason not to try. They congregate with other farmers to create a pessimistic reality that promotes the continued decline of the small farm.

The biggest obstacle many farmers face is a lack of vision. Their words, actions, and beliefs conceal the pathway to success; therefore, they will not succeed because they are opportunity blind and optimism poor.

Anyone can fail at anything at any time. Upsets happen all the time in sports as well as on the farm. When upsets happen, it is better to be in the game than in the stands. Jim Carrey says it this way, *"You can fail at what you don't want, so you might as well take a chance on doing what you love."*

Big ideas provide inspiration. Inspiration generates excitement; this develops purpose and passion, both personally and professionally. An outgrowth of inspiration is creativity, which guides the development of new products, services, processes, and ideas.

Big ideas inspire hope. Hope is a reason to move forward- especially under challenging times. Martin Luther said it this way, *"Everything that is done in this world is done by hope. "* Farming is hope in action. Small farmers hope their seeds become produce, animals become protein, and work becomes profit.

Big ideas express humanity. Expressing humanity means living a meaningful life. Life is more than making a living and paying bills. A small farm must provide an income; however, it should also offer life lessons, enrichment for future generations, and connections with nature.

A farm is a perfect place to express humanity. The way animals are treated reveals kindness. Caring for the land and natural resources demonstrates understanding. Planting hardwood trees for kids or grandkids shows concern for descendants. Expressing humanity is any action that creates a sustainable future for our descendants and their descendants.

Big ideas create prosperity. Big ideas are economic engines allowing people to prosper. The government, Big-Ag, big business, or society is not responsible for the decline of small farms. *The decline in small farms is due to a lack of innovation by small farms*. A small farm with a visionary leader can succeed even in a so-called declining market.

If small farms are going to thrive, they need new and big ideas. All it takes to save many small farms or to start a new farm is just one big idea manifested into a reality. The best competitive advantage and the most valuable business asset are new ideas that lead to profitable products.

Two Small Farm Facts
Some people look at farms and mistakenly think it is simple. Other people look at farming and correctly think the work is hard and dirty. Many people look at farmers as backward and uneducated people. Nearly all people think of farmers as poor.

Other people look at farms and become nostalgic. Some people look at a farm while dreaming of getting back to the land. Other people look at farms with awe and wonder. Many view farms as places of bucolic and pastoral wonder. Nearly all people think of farmers as hard workers.

While some of the above comments may be up for debate, two facts are indisputable. **Fact One: this year, some farmers will fail.** There will be farmers who sell the farm, lose the farm to foreclosure, or will quit for different opportunities. These farmers will pine for the good ole days while blaming their loss on Big-Ag, big box stores, or customers not caring about where their food comes from.

Fact Two: this year, some farmers will succeed. There will be farmers who will buy or lease their neighbor's farm, they will be excited about the future, and they will be thankful that customers care about where their food comes from. These farmers have big ideas for their farms, and they believe small farms provide opportunities.

A good number of these succeeding farmers will be first-time farmers. Many of these new farmers will lack education, expertise, equipment, and experience. These new farmers will try to develop new markets, products, and approaches while generational, established farmers will mock them and take bets with their neighbors about how long these greenhorns will stick around.

Many of these naïve new farmers will succeed. Why will these new farmers be successful, whereas some of the old-timers will fail? These successful farmers, whether new or not, have eight fundamental differences.

1. **Internal Control over External Conditions.** The successful farmer believes they determine their future, and they have control over the future. These farmers recognize the environment has a part to play, but that part is a supporting role.

Like a ship captain, these farmers realize that ocean and weather conditions are imperative, so they monitor the environment and adjust course accordingly.

Competent ship captains take command and determine direction and destination. Responsible small farmers are commanders of life. They make their own decisions, take accountability for their actions, and work harder than people who believe they have little or no control over their life.

2. **Flexibility to change.** Successful farmers acknowledge change happens, whether it is wanted or not. It is a fact the world is evolving, and some people consider it an unpleasant truth. However, the world is a living and dynamic system. Being flexible prepares people for when things do not go as planned, a daily happening for a farmer.

   In farming, there will always be obstacles. When encountering roadblocks, flexibility will get you around that roadblock. You may need to turn around or take a detour, but you still move towards your goal.

3. **Sell a Brand.** This idea will repeat throughout this book. Successful farmers develop brands, and they do not sell a commodity.

4. **Become an Innovator.** Successful small farms use the following 3-Ps of innovation, which are processes, products, and practices. Successful farmers question methods and customer needs and desires while searching for solutions.

Successful farmers grow products people want. In business, what a customer likes is more important than what you like. I do not really like tomatoes, but I grow thousands of tomato plants each year - because it is what people want.

Successful farmers extend their brand to value-added products. Today more than ever, people are looking for locally sourced products and relationships with their farmers. Take advantage of this opportunity.

Successful farms develop and use extraordinary farm practices. Quality farm practices create quality products, and quality products are hard to beat. The marketplace is competitive, and providing quality products is always a great business strategy.

5. **Entrepreneurial drive.** Successful farmers think of themselves as entrepreneurs. Being entrepreneurial is developing a mindset and attitude that actively seeks out opportunities.

   This mindset actively probes the environment while challenging industry norms. An entrepreneurial mindset focuses on innovation, service, creating value, and continuous improvement.

6. **Dare to dream.** The successful farmer exudes vision. Merle Shain states it this way, *"Our strength is in our dreams, and those who do not dare to dream damn themselves."* Successful farmers dare to dream big.

I have talked with farmers who have an objection to every idea or action offered. They are resolved to fail. *Sadly, these farmers are poor in the very worst way; they are poor in dreams.*

On the other hand, I have talked with farmers who have enthusiastically embraced every idea and action offered. They build on these ideas to create new approaches, decisions, and activities. *These farmers may be capital or balance sheet poor, but they are more economically viable because of their dreams.*

7. **Market Seekers.** Unsuccessful farmers wait for customers while offering commodities. Successful farmers are always searching for when and where to sell farm products. One of the worst mistakes a small farmer can make is to depend on the nearest farmers market or the traffic on the road for their income.

   Seek out, customers. Advertise on social media, call people, place ads, and put up a sign! Let people know what you have for sale and how to buy it. Do not be satisfied with just waiting for people to find your farm: seek new customers.

8. **Strive for Significance.** The best farmers plan to be significant. There are three levels of farming. The first and lowest level is survival. Some people are satisfied with growing just enough food to pay some of the bills and to eat.

The second level of farming is fulltime farming. These farmers can quit their off-farm jobs and live off the farm's income. At this level, farmers can afford a few enjoyable things, take a few short vacations, and maybe save a little. For whatever reason, most farmers are satisfied with this level.

The highest level of farming is creating something significant or fulfilling. These farmers want to make a difference. They want to make a difference in society, their community, and their family. People striving for significance are concerned about building something big and leaving a legacy that will serve as an inspiration for future generations.

Working for significance means you have a mission. This mission is a higher calling than just paying the bills. These people have a purpose, and they work to accomplish that mission.

Conclusion

Small farm ideas come from everywhere. Your big farming idea may come from an unexpected place. If you stay open to new ideas, ways of doing things, and learning, you will develop a big plan for your farm. When you create big ideas for your farm, big things will happen, and you will succeed.

What are some of your big ideas for your small farm?

_____

_____

_____

Becoming Destined to Succeed

"It is not in the stars to hold our destiny but in ourselves."
~ **William Shakespeare**

Success starts inside yourself. All impressive accomplishments, all great deeds, and all great farms begin with an individual dream. Everyone wants to be more, do more, and have more, but not everyone puts in the necessary work.

You hold your destiny in your head, heart, and hands. Destiny is not preordained; it is the result of intentional effort. Becoming destined to succeed requires taking a PARE™ approach towards building your small farm through deliberate planning, acting, reflecting, and evolving.

Figure 2.

The PARE™ approach requires breaking things down into manageable and straightforward layers. This approach is based on the dictionary definition of pare, which means to trim away or to make simple. When trying to accomplish big goals, it is easy to make the process complicated; however, grandiose accomplishments need not be complicated.

Planning for a fluid, evolving, and developing future requires believing in your dreams. Eleanor Roosevelt said, "*The future belongs to those who believe in the beauty of their dream.*" Your future and the future of your farm is in your head, heart, and hands.

First, it is in your head. Thinking is the first farming task. All things have a mental and physical creation. Napoleon Hill said it this way, "*All achievements, all earned riches, have their beginning in an idea.*"

Second, it is in your heart because you must love it; farming is a taxing journey. Agriculture provides opportunities to learn and grow from mistakes. Enjoying the ride makes farming both "easy" and enjoyable.

Loving farming means chores are no longer drudgery but a source of enjoyment. When you love farming, what many people find as a struggle you find as exciting, engaging, and enriching. Farming requires unconditional love, the type of love that allows you to work without regard to payment or hours given to the land.

Third, it is in your hands because the work is up to you. **It takes action to succeed**. Once you have a plan, do something daily to make that plan a reality. Even if you do not have land, you can take daily action. That action may be limited to learning something new, but remember all progress is a step forward.

If you have land, do something daily to build your farm. Pick up rocks, pull weeds, feed animals, mend fences, and make plans. Remember, even the smallest step is still progress. These actions transform the mental creation into physical creation and a dream into reality.

Farming never goes as planned, and reflection helps explain why. Reflecting is the process by which you ask yourself what worked, what did not, and why. Contemplation turns failures, missteps, or miscalculations into educational experiences.

Evolve as you go. Darwin said, *"It is not the smartest or strongest organisms that thrive. It is those that are the most responsive to change."* The environment constantly changes and thriving small farms continuously adapt to those changes.

Small farm and homestead profitability is different today than it was just ten years ago. In only ten years, it will be different - again. This struggle is real, and often crippling, especially for multigenerational family farms whose current owners wage war to maintain the status quo. If you want to build a farm that stands the test of time and build something to leave behind to your children and grandchildren, it must evolve.

Conclusion

Becoming destined to succeed requires creating the future. The PARE model is a process that creates a future of your design. Each moment of each day brings us closer to or pushes us further from our dreams. We must be intentional with plans and actions for big accomplishments to become a reality.

Becoming a Brand

*"Produce and protein come from the fields.
Brands come from the heart."* ~ **Jason McClure**

Build a brand. A brand is much more than a logo, symbol, or mark. *A brand is an emotional connection with customers.* A brand is all the qualities that make a farm special, and it is the most critical marketing pursuit for any farm (or business).

People taking pride in their farm's products, practices, and purposes create valuable brands. It seems obvious to say, but all enterprises grow or die because of their reputation. In simplest terms, an attractive brand brings customers to the farm, and an unattractive brand repels customers. As a matter of fact, most products and services are purchased solely because of the brand name.

When it comes to the importance of building strong brands, small farms are no different from any other businesses. When people in your community think of quality farm products, your farm should be the farm they think of first. The only way small farms can create a sustainable brand is by delivering on customer service and creating valuable products. A brand is a farm's reputation and its position in its community as well as in the marketplace.

When a small farm builds a great brand, it creates repeat customers who become advocates. When branding, think in terms of human traits and qualities. This process creates an emotional appeal and establishes connections while giving a human touch to your farm. Most importantly, a brand provides a small farm personality and voice.

Ten types of farm brand personalities:
1. **Adventurous** – This personality focuses on experiences. An adventurous farm brand provides customers new and different experiences that are exciting and enriching. For a small farm, this can include things like farm tours, events, or activities.

2. **Serious** – This personality is straight forward and no-nonsense. In business, this person is more transactional than relational. We all know people that do not like small talk, and this brand appeals to those people. This personality tends to be direct and dry.

3. **Humorous** - This personality is funny and relational. A farm with this brand uses wit and comedy to make their points. This farm is lighthearted and will often poke fun at itself. The customer who is attracted to the serious brand will most likely avoid this farm. This farm tends to be a fun place to visit.

4. **Eco-friendly** – This mission-driven personality cares about the environment or other social issues. Customers attracted to this personality follow environmental concerns, are mindful about the raising, storing, and transportation of products, and are less concerned about price and appearance. These customers purchase organically and naturally grown products and are willing to pay a premium for locally sourced farm products.

5. **Ruggedness** – This personality is tough, weathered, and principled. This personality represents endurance and timeless principles. These customers are hardworking people who may have blue-collar roots and enjoy working with their hands.

6. **Quirky** – This personality is idiosyncratic. These people are food bloggers or food connoisseurs, searching for interesting and perhaps strange food. Quirky customers prefer unique or different foods and are great candidates for heritage proteins or heirloom veggies.

7. **Expert** – This personality takes pride in their expertise and wants others to know how smart they are. Experts have comprehensive knowledge about a subject, in this case, farming. Curious customers and early adopters are attracted to this personality.

8. **Soulful** – This personality is expressive, emotional, and moving. A soulful brand attracts highly passionate people. This brand places more emphasis on spiritual qualities than they do on what many small farmers would consider "rational" conditions.

9. **Bold** – This personality is larger than life; they take risks. A bold brand makes big claims and then works to deliver on those claims. Customers who put a premium on quality products are attracted to this brand.

10. **Simplistic** – This brand personality has a simple approach to things. This brand is traditional and straightforward with a no-frill, almost dull offering. A simplistic brand will have black and white, forthright labels. Customers attracted to this type of brand are nostalgic and sentimental with a longing for the good ole days. This population is a reflective and wistful group who are more impressed with the basic design than sophisticated packaging, mainly used by mega-corporations.

Each personality has its pros and cons; your farm's values, vision, and mission statement will guide you in the development of your farm's persona. The best identity for your farm is the personality that feels right to you. You may be a mix of personalities – and that is okay – but you are likely to "major" in one.

When picking your farm's personality, be sincere. According to Jean Giraudoux, "*The secret of success is sincerity.*" With the farm to table and locally grown movements, customers are searching for sincerity and authenticity.

Just as different people are attracted to different personalities, the same is correct with brand personalities. Not everyone is going to be a customer. Besides, not everyone who buys your product is a customer. I define a customer as a person who buys a product and has a long-term relationship with my farm; a consumer makes a one time or casual purchase.

Customers are more likely to purchase a brand if its personality is like their own. Each media attracts a specific personality, and your advertising dollars need to align with the media audience and your brand's personality.

Brand Personality Worksheet
If your brand was a person, how would describe him or her?

_____

_____

Would your brand be a man or a woman? Young or old? Friendly or edgy? Smart or funny? Simple or eclectic?

_____

_____

_____

Where would your brand shop? What sort of farm products are they looking for? What sort or level of service do they expect?

_____

_____

_____

What value are you going to provide for your customer?
_____

_____

_____

What is your core verbal message?
_____

_____

_____

Describe your business in 3 to 5 sentences:

_____

_____

_____

Write your social media bio.

_____

_____

_____

What is your farm's purpose?

_____

_____

_____

What actions are you going to take to fulfill that purpose?

_____

_____

_____

What are your areas of specialty? What is your farm going to major in?

_____

_____

What is your brand? What are your products, services, and who are your core customers?

_____

_____

_____

Conclusion

It is much better to sell a branded product than a commodity. Branded products sell for a premium, earning extra profit for the same amount of work. Brand building requires work, but it is worth it.

A strong brand is a great weapon to push back against the onslaught of misinformation, inferior products, and corporate greed from the mega-corporations who are seeking to destroy you. Also, a brand is beneficial for customers. It lets customers know they are buying quality, locally grown products from a trusted source.

Becoming a Dynamic Farm

"Life is a series of natural and spontaneous changes. Don't resist them; that only creates sorrow. Let reality be reality. Let things flow naturally forward in whatever way they like." ~ **Lao Tzu**

Seasons change. The weather is a dynamic system with patterns. Seasons evolve through the year as spring turns into summer, summer turns into fall, fall turns into winter, and winter turns back into spring. However, each spring is different from the last; there have never been two exact seasons, years, or days.

The weather is a chaotic system. Farmers know this, which is why they plan the year's work based on the changing seasons. Each season requires specific work, tasks, and activities.

The economic system is chaotic. Never have two days, weeks, months, years, or decades existed with the same economic conditions. The economy has peaks and valleys. Besides, whether the economy is good or bad, there will always be farms that do well and farms that will fail.

As a farmer, you need to adjust to the current economic situation. It is imperative to prepare for bad times so you can survive them. Small farms that plan for economic downturns gain new customers and expand their operations as producers drop out of the marketplace.

The economy is changing and evolving.
Farmers know this, but not all farmers act on this. It is interesting how the same farmer who cooperates with the environment will become an obstinate energy waster when it comes to economic forces or market demands.

Economic forces are powerful, which is why it is wise to work with these forces instead of against them. It is like operating a sailboat. A sailor has no control over the wind, but a skilled sailor can arrive at his or her destination by adjusting their sails.

Just as a sailor has no control over the wind, you have no control over the economy. You do have control over your response. More importantly, you can be proactive and adapt in anticipation of future changes.

I recently had a conversation with a farmer complaining about the "*liberal agenda.*" According to this person, the liberal push for "*organically grown*" food is hurting farmers' efficiencies. He may be right in that producing organically grown food is less efficient. He is wrong for complaining and criticizing customers for expressing what they want.

The problem with this farmer is he is taking an operations approach to farming. An operations approach works best in a commodity-based industry were commodities sell at a market-clearing price. Therefore, if you are a commodity farmer, factory farmer, or large-scale processor, the operations approach maybe your best option. In that case, this book is not for you.

Small farms must take a market approach with their business. It is futile to push back against changing customer preferences. I believe in the free market, and I think market-driven economies provide the best efficiencies. I also understand customers cannot be compelled to buy products they do not want, desire, or like.

Farm operations are essential because the best marketing in the world is worthless if you do not have a product to sell. On the other hand, you can have the best farm practices and still not produce what customers want.

Small farms, if they want to thrive, must take a market-driven approach towards building their businesses. A marketing approach focuses on building relationships with consumers and transforming commodities into branded products.

This means being customer-centric and not farmer-centric. Being customer-centric recognizes the customer is the most necessary person in any business relationship. Growing small farm profitability requires a shift from focusing only on operations to concentrating on marketing with a clear emphasis on customer needs.

As an example, dairy farmers have been going out of business for decades. Each news report is the same story with a different family. A family farm loses a contract; during the interview, the farmer talks about decreased demand, lower revenue, and increased expenses as the reasons for shutting down.

These farmers recognized economic forces existed and did nothing different. Many times, they or the reporter will quote a USDA statistic that states dairy farms had decreased from 83,000 in 2000 to 40,000 in 2018. It is shocking and staggering that this specific industry has lost over half its producers in 18 years, but, once again, this is not new. It has been happening for at least a generation.

However, not all dairy farmers are going out of business. There are dairy farmers that are growing and gaining ground. For example, the Marcoot Jersey Creamery, a seventh-generation family-owned dairy farm in Greenville, Illinois, produces and sells artesian and farmstead cheese either online or in their farm store located on their property.

This family recognized the industry was changing. Instead of producing more milk at lower prices, they shifted their focus to the farm to table movement by designing a high-end artesian quality cheese.

They are not the only dairy farm bucking the trend and doing well. The White River Creamery in Northwest Arkansas is a first-generation dairy farm producing artesian cheese. Like the Marcoot family, they sell their product online, at the farm, as well as wholesale. Unlike the Marcoot family, who had a family farm, the White River Creamery entered a declining industry to build a successful niche from scratch.

The difference between the dairy farmers going out of business and the dairy farmers expanding their business is their responses to market conditions. The dairy farmers going out of business are static, stationary, and stagnant.

They keep approaching new problems with old ways of thinking and, as a result, they are going out of business. Instead of trying new approaches, products, or practices, they just do more of what they have always done.

The thriving dairy farmers are evolving to meet the needs of a dynamic marketplace and changing customer preferences. These farmers realize that the best tradition is not some outdated method of doing business or an outdated farm practice. Still, the best tradition is having a "can do" mindset backed by gumption.

Dynamic Small Farms

Being a dynamic small farm means adjusting to environmental changes. Change happens moment by moment. Entropy is the norm - not order and predictability. Many people mistakenly believe that systems are static, dependable, and predictable when the opposite is true.

Most people mistakenly associate entropy with chaos and disarray. The better way to view entropy is as freedom from rules, norms, and industry expectations. Entropy releases energy in new directions, fuels new ideas, and discovers new opportunities. Entropy makes it possible for new farmers to succeed where old farmers have failed.

Economic entropy allows farmers with new ideas to replace farmers with old ideas. I do not think it is sad that family farms are declining. I think it is unfortunate that family farms are not evolving and growing. The founders of these farms had gumption, ideas, and drive - something the current owners seem to lack.

Conclusion

As a farmer, you must adjust. Your farm is your dream, and for the vision to thrive, you need customers. Becoming a dynamic farm means growing products and providing the services people want. Being dynamic or progressive means being willing to accept, adjust, and adapt to changes in the marketplace.

Becoming Entrepreneurial

"The entrepreneur is essentially a visualizer and actualizer. He can visualize something, and when he visualizes it, he sees exactly how to make it happen." ~ **Robert L. Schwartz**

Entrepreneurs are America's driving force. This segment is made up of the pioneers, innovators, and risk-takers. They create jobs for people, value for their customers, and are the engineers of their own realities.

Thriving, small farmers are entrepreneurial. This trait requires being creative when developing products and services as well as actively marketing farm products. Almost anyone can grow vegetables or raise animals. Fewer people can create a vision of what to do with those products beyond the obvious. Even fewer can put that vision into action.

Entrepreneurs turn ideas into realities. Being an entrepreneur is a mindset as much as it is a practice. Anyone can be entrepreneurial. All it takes is developing the following fifteen entrepreneurial traits:

Trait 1: Vison. All entrepreneurial endeavors start with a vision. Develop an idea of what kind of farm you are going to build and what it takes to create or grow that farm. The more grandiose, the better. Thinking big is both free and freeing. There is no cost associated with thinking big; however, there is an opportunity cost to small-mindedness and limited thinking.

Trait 2: Engineer your Reality. Engineering your future means creating your future. To do this requires planning for tomorrow, next week, next year, and the next decade. Dreaming big and bold is terrific, but it takes workable plans to pull that dream from the realm of the abstract into the physical world.

Trait 3: Motivation. Motivation is the drive to do things today, knowing the payoff will be in the future. Having and lacking motivation is the difference between success and failure for most small farmers.

Doing easy things are easy, but successful farming is never without obstacles. Thriving agriculture is always hard, and it will still require motivation. Motivation is the drive that will get the hard things done on time and done correctly.

Trait 4: Discipline. Discipline kicks in when motivation wears thin. Discipline provides the courage to do things that need to be done, when they need to be done, the way they need to be done. Successful farmers have physical, emotional, and financial discipline.

Farms do not stop because of rainy, snowy, and windy days with extreme temperatures. Chores still need attending to, requiring physical discipline.

Animals require culling, vetting, or putting down. It requires emotional discipline to make hard decisions and to take demanding actions. Raising animals requires loving them while at the same time recognizing their purpose and that at some point, for some reason, they may need to be put down.

As a farmer, there will be tools that will make your job easier. Being financially disciplined means putting off purchasing those tools until you can afford them. Thomas Jefferson gave the best advice on this topic when he said, *"Never spend your money before you have it."*

Trait 5: Resourcefulness. Napoleon Hill said, *"A resourceful person will always make an opportunity."* As a farmer, you need to develop the talent to do the best you can with what you have. Remember, American expansion occurred because people settling new areas replaced resources with resourcefulness. That same spirit can expand your farm.

Resourceful, in this context, means seeing or creating an opportunity within your current constraints. To develop resourcefulness, consistently take inventory of your assets, including your knowledge or skills, and make a list of how to turn those assets into money.

Every item on a small farm has multiple uses. For example, used baling twine is excellent for fence-mending, tie-downs, tomato staking, and 100 other applications. Scrap lumber can find its way into building projects. When possible, use rocks in place of blocks. Use tree limbs for fence stays. The only limit to resourcefulness is imagination.

Small farms come with a limited budget and unlimited needs. Stretch the budget by always naming ten other uses for whatever you have in front of you. For me, this creativity is one of the joys of farming and a mindset that helps the bank account.

Trait 6: Take Action. An ounce of action is worth more than a pound of planning. Anyone can plan and talk about things. *Planning is essential, but taking action is more important*. I agree with Bo Bennet, who says, "*A dream becomes a goal when action is taken toward its achievement.*"

Trait 7: Focus on Details. Focus on the little things. Many times, it's the little things that will sidetrack your day. A missing tractor pin, forgetting to grease the tractor, or forgetting to lock a gate will set forth a series of unfortunate events that will change your current priorities.

Attention to detail also extends to customers. Customers remember the little things. When I sell produce, I inspect it one last time as I hand it to the customer. If something is less than perfect, I replace it. Whenever I do this, the customer thanks me, and most of them buy from me again.

When I sell meat, I double-check the weight, and I always make sure that they get a little more than what they expect. I inspect the packaging for imperfections, and I have the same response. When people give you money for a product, they reward this attention to detail by becoming a loyal customer.

Trait 8: Take Risks. Undertaking something original and innovative is perilous. Many farmers are risk-averse, which is confusing given the nature of the business. Farming has always been an uncertain enterprise. Many daily factors are outside of the farmers' control; yet, when it comes to some new business ideas, traditional farmers are often the most reluctant to try.

In business, the most significant risk is not to take a chance. The world changes daily, and it is essential to anticipate and adjust to those changes. Joy Mango says, *"Don't be afraid to have a reality check. Taking risks is OK, but you must be realistic."*

Trait 9. Continuous Learning. You can never be too smart. Look at what small farms are doing both nationwide and worldwide. The internet is a great tool to use for discovering new or different farm practices, products, or projects for your farm.

According to Tena Desae, the key to learning and success is *"Stay positive and happy. Work hard and don't give up hope. Be open to criticism and keep learning. Surround yourself with happy, warm, and genuine people."* Criticism is an often overlooked and painful source of learning. When people are critical, think about what they are saying and why they are saying it.

Many people will be harsh on your dreams because they do not have their own ambitions. Others will build you up and offer you good advice. If you are open, you can learn something from both groups.

With farming, you will never learn everything. Every season I learn new things about the cattle I raise and the produce I have grown. Every season I keep learning and growing.

Trait 10: Create Rules. Every industry, including farming, has unwritten rules that provide a framework of how people are expected to interact and behave. These rules favor established players and support the status quo, which is fine if you are at the top.

Entrepreneurs are rule-breakers. Rule breakers reshape industries. For example, Amazon shaped the way people bought books. TV entertainment consumption was changed by Netflix, the company that invented binging. Uber changed the way people get around cities. Airbnb changed the way people find lodging. **You can change the way people buy locally grown food.**

Entrepreneurs create new rules. I believe small farms need to be thinking like Crowd Cow, Swanson's, or Blue Apron. These companies use technology wisely. I feel small farms using the same technology and techniques can grow into large businesses.

Do not limit yourself by antiquated rules. Farmers markets, roadside stands, and/or farm stores are fantastic. However, they have limitations. Create new rules and new ways of interacting with customers, and you will be the next industry leader.

Trait 11: Efficacy. Efficacy is from the Latin verb *efficere,* which means, *"to work out, accomplish."* To have efficacy means you have the power to succeed. Efficacy comes from inner strength and self-awareness, and it provides a realistic road map towards a goal or an objective.

Efficacy is more than belief. *It is a belief backed with competence.* Without competence, it is delusional thinking. To have real efficacy, you must have task knowledge combined with the understanding your farm's success is possible.

The essential part of efficacy is the action of working out the required steps and actions needed for accomplishment. Efficacy allows you to identify and eliminate obstacles, set priorities and put forward the effort.

Trait 12: Optimism. Thomas Jefferson said, *"I like the dreams of the future better than the history of the past."* The future is coming, and you must be optimistic about it. Entrepreneurs believe in their future because they create it. Entrepreneurial optimism moves markets, builds new industries, and generates wealth.

Trait 13: Leadership. Success in a grueling and challenging industry, such as farming, requires visionary leadership. These leaders inspire, motivate, and influence people. Also, they provide corporate vision and strategic direction while establishing priorities. Most importantly, leadership creates a farm's culture: a way of life.

These FAST™ principles can make you a leader.

- **Following**. Before you can effectively lead, you need to know how to follow. If you have ever had a job, you have been a follower. If you have ever been to school, you know how to follow. Knowing how to follow is one reason people from humble beginnings tend to do move up further than people who started higher up on the social-economic ladder.
- **Accountability**. Followers develop into leaders by taking ownership of things. Instead of waiting for instructions, they take the initiative and do something. Accountability is being both responsible and proactive.
- **Standards**. Ray Kroc says, *"The quality of a leader is reflected by the standards they set for themselves."* When a leader settles for good enough, then good enough is the standard. When a leader pushes for great, then great is the standard.
- **Together**. Leadership is getting people to work together and getting people to buy into your vision of the future. Small farms are hard work, and for them to grow, it is going to take people working together for a common goal.

Trait 14: Be Artistic. Entrepreneurs are economic artists. Like an artist, entrepreneurs combine skills, knowledge, and imagination to create something new. Artists see the potential in ordinary objects. Building on that potential, artists can create something of beauty and worthy of admiration.

Small farmers need to think of themselves as artists. Small farms are places of splendor. Farmers turn wild and rugged landscapes into places of wonder. Charles Warner said, "*A great artist can paint a great picture on a small canvas.*" I interpret this to mean a great farmer can build a great business on a small farm.

Farming is often too rational, mechanistic, and impassioned. Frequently people live life in the same way. When we take an artist's approach to life, we start to see the beauty in the world, express our humanity, and design a fulfilling life.

Trait 15: Become Great. Entrepreneurs focus on greatness. Jim Collins opens his book *From Good to Great* with the phrase, "*Good is the enemy of great.*" Many people do not achieve greatness because things are good, and they get comfortable with things. When things are good, it is easy to go with the flow, become complacent, and rest on one's laurels.

Being good just feels right. It brings safety and security. It provides a sense of comfort and control. With a good business in place, it is tempting not to rock the boat but to continue to go with the flow.

However, smooth sailing is the most dangerous situation for any business. Smooth sailing teaches the next generation that success is always going to be easy. The best way to prepare a small farm for the next generation is to be relentlessly committed to great.

Conclusion

It is going to take an entrepreneurial vision to change the tide of declining farms. This change is going to happen on one small farm at a time. Approach your small farm with entrepreneurial imagination, drive, and creativity, and it will thrive. It may not succeed overnight, but it will one day blossom.

Becoming a Farm Visionary

"When you have a vision, it affects your attitude. Your attitude is optimistic rather than pessimistic." ~ **Charles R. Swindoll**

Industry visionaries defy the status quo by writing their own rules. Anyone can join any industry and survive by learning the principles and norms of that industry. However, not anyone can reshape an industry according to his or her goals.

The farming industry is inundated with antiquated practices, a reason many generational family farms struggle. The USDA reinforces this by providing pamphlets, programs, and educational opportunities to train and educate all farmers in the exact same way.

The result is a very sterile industry, void of innovation. Could you imagine this approach in any other industry? What if every restaurant was the exact same? What if every gas station was the same? What if every shoe had the exact same design with no variation? This would result in a bland, lifeless, and complacent world.

Many people talk about standardization as if it should be an industry goal. The problem with standardization is it weakens innovation, which is the best source of economic development and prosperity. When farmers buy into this standardization trap, they develop commodities and become price takers instead of price makers.

Dare to be different. In business, differentiation is a good thing. Differentiation is a process of change and growth. Just as biological systems grow and adapt, economic systems must evolve and adapt. More importantly, industries within commercial systems must grow and adapt. Experimenting with new crops, services, and processes allows customers to state their preferences by their purchases while allowing daring farmers to earn more profit.

Best Practices for Small Farms: Become a Visionary

Best Practice 1: Innovate. Innovative products or services provide small farms, more customers who are willing to pay more money for farm products. Just as with any other industry, new farmers who innovate will replace farmers who do not innovate.

The best innovators collaborate with others. The best group to work with is your customers. The worst people to collaborate with are established farmers who have been using the same methods and selling the same products for generations.

The marketplace is evolving, and farms that stand the test of time will grow with the market. This approach does not mean that you change your core values, principles, or beliefs. It means you focus on creating value for the customer.

Best Practice 2: Customer Value. Farm visionaries focus on customer value. To become a farm visionary, always ask yourself what your customer wants and how you can supply what they want at a fair profit.

Best Practice 3: Anticipate Customer Needs. Customer experience limits expectations, wants, and desires. Visionaries think of customer wants or needs before customers they know want or need it.

At one point, I had a phone attached to a wall. Its sole purpose was to make and receive phone calls. Today, my phone is in my pocket. In addition to making calls, it sends texts, takes pictures, produces videos, connects to the web, tracks my location, and plays games.

As a customer with a phone connected to the wall, I had no idea that those other things were an option. My experience with the phone limited my expectations. As a matter of fact, if you asked me if I wanted a phone to take pictures, I would have thought you were crazy.

The same is spot-on for farm products. There are uses for farm products that customers have not thought of, and if you think of these uses, you can profit. The only limit to creating new products and services is your imagination.

Best Practice 4: Think Like an Outsider. Outsiders question practices and challenge paradigms. They apply new ways of thinking to old problems. These crazy outsiders bring to life these words from Abert Einstein, *"We cannot solve our problems with the same thinking we used when we created them."* This way of thinking is why in many industries, not just farming, it is outsiders who come in and shake things up.

Many farmers have self-imposed limitations called traditions. It is tempting to follow these traditions; however, these traditions belong to other people. The primary problem with tradition is it limits thinking and stifles creativity while creating a reluctance to try new and fresh ideas.

Best Practice 5: Do not Accept Other People's Limitations. Chase accomplishment as if there are no limits. Do not let others tell you what you can or cannot accomplish. You should not settle for less, just because others have settled for less. The most significant and most challenging barriers to overcome are the barriers of the mind. Chuck Yeager said it this way, *"Breaking the sound barrier wasn't about some invisible wall in the sky, but the barriers in our own minds."*

You are creating your future. Yes, there are resource limitations, but the most significant barrier is what you believe to be true. Follow the advice of Michael Jordan, who said, *"Limits, like fears, are just an illusion."*

Best Practice 6: Move Forward. Move towards your goal: not away from it. If there is an obstacle, move towards it. The closer you are to the problem, the closer you are to the solution.

When farming, there will be setbacks, obstacles, and failures. Treat each of these events as learning experiences. Henry Ford said it best when he said, *"Failure is simply the opportunity to begin again, this time more intelligently."*

Best Practice 7: Have a Bias for Action. Do something even if it is wrong. Do not let your lack of experience or education slow your action. If you act and fail, you are a step closer to success because you just figured out what not to do. *Visionaries take action*. You can do something daily to move your farm forward, even if that something is learning something new.

Best Practice 8: Define Your Own Reality. Words create reality. Word choice sculpts others' perceptions of your farm. Therefore, when talking about your farm, use words that will unleash its potential. Word calculation controls thoughts, which regulates behavior, action, and outcomes.

Defining reality is a matter of interpretation and managing meanings. Many people do not actively manage connotations; they just accept other people's definitions as reality. Successful farmers manage their own meanings for their own purposes. When dealt with a setback, it becomes a learning event and an opportunity to prove their success principles work instead of viewing it as a failure or viewing themselves as a loser.

Best Practice 9: Scalability. Small farms must grow to thrive. A mentor once said, "*If you are going to be rich, you must have something making you money while you sleep.*" This fact is true because one person can only work so many hours a day and can do only so much.

Scalability means depending on others. Growth requires teamwork. As a leader, you are going to have to train, delegate, and manage people. This process requires letting go of things and not micromanage every little detail.

Scalability means growth. Having a team allows individuals to work on tasks, projects, or programs that complement their strengths and benefit the farm.

Best Practice 10: **Swim-up Stream**. Do not follow the crowd. Work to make sure your farm is a standout farm. A common mistake many people make is to strive toward becoming part of an industry's "in crowd." This approach is problematic as it puts the focus on the industry when the focus should be on the customer.

Frequently, becoming an industry leader means your ego is taking precedence over your customers. Many prioritize news headlines and social media likes over the needs of their customers. Instead, follow Sam Walton's lead, who said, "*Swim upstream. Go the other way. Ignore conventional wisdom.*"

Conclusion

Small farm success is directly proportional to the vision of its owner. Visionary farmers are optimistic, and optimism is a requirement for success in any business. Farmers who lack vision are pessimistic and are their biggest competitors. Therefore, develop a vision for your farm and work daily to turn that vision into reality.

Becoming Customer-centric

Make a customer, not a sale. ~ ***Katherine Barchetti***

A common phrase says, *"If you have eaten today, thank a farmer."* That phrase is harmful, especially to small farmers who believe it. The problem with that phrase is it makes the farmer the most crucial person in the transaction. The most important person in any business equation is the customer.

For the bulk of human history, people have raised their own food, and I believe people can grow their own food again. Many farmers mistakenly believe customers are dependent upon them when, in fact, the opposite is true.

If you enjoy owning land, farming, and interacting with nature, ***you should be thanking customers for making that possible***. Customers do not need farmers for food. Customers need farmers for convenience!

Farmers provide a product and service that allows people to spend their free time doing something other than raising food. This service enables people to pursue careers, education, art, leisure, or a host of other activities. When farmers grow food for people, they are not keeping people from starving. Farmers are providing customers time, energy, and freedom to pursue other activities.

If farms disappeared, people would adapt. People would turn to hunting, fishing, and gathering. People would then start to grow their own food. On the other hand, if your customers disappeared, could you adapt or survive?

I get a lot of criticism for this saying that, but I stand by my belief that customers should be at the heart of what a farmer does. **Being customer-centric means implementing these four best customer-centric practices.**

Four Best Customer-centric Practices for Small Farms

Best Practice 1: Create an Experience. Customer experience drives processes, practices, and products. The customer experience includes all the ways people interact with your product - the taste, packaging, and delivery. It is much better to provide a great product while apologizing for the price than to give away an inferior product while apologizing for quality.

People will complain about the price and even tolerate a slightly higher price. However, they will not tolerate inferior products. If you consistently produce high-quality products, you will be successful. It might take a while, but you will be successful.

Best Practice 2: Perception Creates Reality. A customer's perception of your farm is vital for your farm's sustainability. Customers bring money into the farm, and for this reason alone, it is crucial, critical, and integral to managing it.

Managing perception and creating reality is about storytelling. People love stories. All industries have businesses that owe their success to their storytelling. The best marketing and brand building revolves around stories and how words form, shape, and guide reality.

Customer perception starts with your opinion, attitudes, and beliefs. If you perceive your products as superior and back up that belief with action, customers will believe it, too. If you believe your products are no different from anyone else's, your customers will also think about it the same way.

Best Practice 3: Exceed Expectations. Exceeding customer expectations separates you from the competition. As my grandfather used to say, *"There isn't a traffic jam on the extra mile."* He was right; though many agree with this concept, only a few will act.

Best Practice 4: Understand Emotions. Essentially, this means identifying and uncovering customers' emotional needs, desires, and their rationale behind those needs. Virtually every purchase is an emotional decision. We all purchase products to make us feel better about ourselves for a variety of reasons. Then we all use logic to justify those purchases through a process called retro sensemaking.

Successful small farm marketers understand the emotional appeal of their farm products. The goal is to make customers happy and to feel as if they are contributing to something. As you market your small farm, keep in mind many people like to buy local, want to support the local economy, save the environment, and want to know their farmer.

To make this emotional connection, treat customers like friends, invest time in the relationship, and, most importantly, treat customers as fellow humans.

Conclusion

The customer is the farm's most important stakeholder. Without customers, finances evaporate, resources disappear, and the farm dream vanishes. Successful farms develop a customer base. I find it is best to start with one customer, take care of that customer, and then add more customers.

Small Farm Advertising: 11 Proven Strategies

*"Good marketing makes the company look smart. Great marketing makes the customer feel smart." ~ **Joe Chernov***

Marketing is the difference between selling a featureless commodity and a valuable branded product. For too long, farmers have been content with selling commodities at market prices while complaining about how retailers and processors get rich off their hard work.

The goal of marketing is to make your farm products stand out in a crowded marketplace. Marketing allows you to find, build, and deepen relationships with customers willing to pay a premium for a premium product.

Marketing drives your brand, and your brand creates an emotional attachment with your customer. You work hard to create great products. Therefore, it makes sense to let the world know about your products. Let them know why your product is so valuable! Marketing shares your confidence in your work.

Small Farm Advertising Strategy 1: Find Your Voice

*"Your time is limited, so don't waste it living someone else's life. Don't be trapped by dogma - which is living with the results of other people's thinking. Don't let the noise of others' opinions drown out your own inner voice. And most important, dare to follow your heart and intuition." ~ **Steve Jobs***

A great thing about farming is you decide how to farm. You can be organic or not. You can be all-natural or not. You can use old or modern growing methods. You can mix and match any of the above, take things to an extreme, or use moderation. The choice is yours.

Farming is an opportunity to develop and express your voice. **Developing your voice requires confidence in your values.** Stephen Covey defines values as self-selected beliefs, and this book utilizes Covey's definition. One of the most important business (and personal) decisions a person makes is their selection of values.

Roy Disney advocated, *"It's not hard to make decisions when you know what your values are."* Intentionally selecting values makes decision making much more natural, and this, in turn, aligns actions with values. This alignment creates credibility, which goes a long way when brand building.

Intentionality must guide the value selection process.
Wayne Dyer warns, *"Intention creates reality."* Values and
beliefs are the most basic building blocks of outcomes,
which is why selecting values requires diligence and
precision. The best advice is to be authentic during the
process of selecting values.

Being authentic in a fake world makes you a standout.
There is no need to be something you are not. Being
authentic requires being brave and living up to your core
set of values. Andie MacDowell puts it this way, *"when you
are authentic, you create a certain energy; people want to be
around you because you are unique."*

It is a good business practice to be authentic. This practice
attracts more customers, builds goodwill with suppliers,
and attracts higher-quality employees. People can and will
copy your farm's products and traditions, but they cannot
copy your authenticity.

Authenticity is a core leadership trait. You are your farm's
leader. All too often, farmers complain about the quality of
their employees. Great employees are the result of training
and development based on an organization's core values.
Your farm's corporate profits serve as a guide for their
behavior, just as it serves as a guide for your action. When
you hire employees, choose new people for value fit and
not technical skills. Arte Nathan says it this way, *"You can't
teach employees to smile. They have to smile before you hire
them."* Use this as a reminder that it is easier to train for
skill than to teach values.

Your values give you a voice. To help vocalize your values answer the following five questions:

1. Why do I farm?

_____

_____

_____

_____

2. What current farm trends do I believe in?

_____

_____

_____

_____

3. What current farm trends do I think are ineffective?

_____

_____

_____

_____

4. What can I do to be a leader in positive trends?

_____

_____

_____

_____

5. What trend(s) would I like to start?

_____

_____

_____

_____

Corporate values guide the development of vision and mission statements. A vision statement describes an idealized reality, and a mission statement describes what you are going to do to make that idealized reality an actualized reality.

Vision and mission statements are more than marketing statements. They are working definitions to guide your farm's practices, processes, and procedures. When choosing values, select 3 to 6 values, a number consistent among consultants and researchers. Too few values make it seem as if you do not stand for anything, allowing room for ambiguity. Too many values are hard to remember and difficult to execute.

As you pick farm values, be self-reflective, ask why you chose that value. Define what it means to you, what it means for your customer, and whether it is authentic or a societal expectation. Here is a template for this exercise. The appendix has a list of sample values to aid in your brainstorming.

Value	My Definition	Customer Benefit	Authentic Value or A Societal Expectation?

Creating a Vision Statement
Your vision statement is a clarifying statement of your farm's future. This must communicate what your farm is aspiring to become. Build your vision statement by defining the following 3Ps:

Purpose – What is your farm's purpose?

_____

_____

_____

_____

Passion – What is your farm's passion?

_____

_____

_____

_____

Pursuit – What ideals is your farm going to pursue?

_____

_____

_____

_____

Using the ideas above, what is your farm's vision? It needs to be concise.

_____

_____

_____

_____

Creating a Mission Statement:
Your mission statement explains what you do, how do you do it, and who you do it for. The mission communicates corporate values while inspiring customers and employees. As you write your mission statement, answer the following questions:

1. What do you farm, and why?

_____

_____

_____

_____

2. Who are your customers (what kind of people are looking for your farm products)?

_____

_____

_____

_____

3. How do you differ from competitors (think retail stores, farm stores, roadside stands, restaurants, and other farms)?

_____

_____

_____

_____

4. What underlying philosophies guide your farm operations?

_____

_____

_____

_____

5. What is your farm mission statement?

_____

_____

_____

_____

Conclusion

Your voice expresses your farm's values, communicates your vision and mission, and gives expression to your brand. Intentionally build your farm's voice, and people will respond enthusiastically.

Your farm is your voice. Your farm's practices, products, and procedures allow you to share your beliefs with the world. Therefore, be intentional, purposeful, and authentic as you develop and use that voice.

The appendix offers sample values, mission statements, and vision statements to help guide the development of your voice. Do not use these tools to mimic other people, but use them as a brainstorming tool to develop your unique place in the market.

Small Farm Advertising Strategy 2: Understand the Competition

"If you're a true warrior, competition doesn't scare you. It makes you better." ~ **Andrew Whitworth**

Understanding your competition makes you a better farmer. There are two ways to define who competitors are. First, the competition is any provider of any type of food, a broad category, and daunting in scope. Secondly, the competition is other small farms - especially those you admire. This is a much narrower, less daunting, and educational task.

Many people think of business competition as a head-to-head confrontation. That business is war, you must destroy the competition, and I can have more by running some other person out of business. This zero-sum or win-lose mindset is more limiting than it is expansive.

This is the *scarcity mindset* in action. The person with this mindset believes resources are limited, and the only way to get more is for someone else to get less. This mindset keeps people in poverty, makes it difficult to collaborate, and prohibits business and personal growth.

The market for farm to table products is enormous and few, if any, customers will have a binary choice between you and another farm. In the rare situation where the option is binary, be gracious with the customer and the other person; this provides a much better feeling than resentment.

Ramana Maharshi explains it this way, *"If you approach the ocean with a cup, you can only take away a cupful; if you approach it with a bucket, you can take away a bucketful."* The person approaching the ocean with a cup has a scarcity mindset, and the person approaching the sea with a bucket has an abundance mindset. Be the person with the bucket.

Industries working against your values and interests are the enemy. There is nothing wrong with wanting to take on the interests of corporate America or industrial Ag. This approach positions a small farm as an ethical provider of quality products and as someone earnestly concerned about the local economy and environment.

Understanding your competition is a way to learn from other people's successes and failures. Most small farmers are willing to share insights and practices with other farmers, though there will always be outliers.

Select at least ten small farms you admire and use the template below as a guide to analyzing them.

Statement, Item or Question	Response
Name of Farm	

Location	
Web Address	
Products or Services	
Mission Statement	
Vision Statement	
Values or Value Statement	
Website or Social Media	
What do you like?	
What do you dislike?	
What can you do better?	
What can they do better?	
How long have they been in operation?	
What you do differently? And why?	
What you do the same? And why?	

Where do they sell products?	
Who buys their products? Restaurants, Stores, Families, income level, demographic information, etc.	

Conclusion

Life is not a zero-sum game. The marketplace is large enough for many people to succeed, and the overall economy does better when more people are reaching their goals. So do not limit yourself by operating out of a scarcity mindset; instead, expand opportunities by working out of an abundance mindset.

This strategy is called "understand the competition" and not "beat the competition" for a reason. Understanding the competition allows you to learn from the success and failure of others. In doing this, you create opportunities, expand boundaries, and grow knowledge.

Small Farm Advertising Strategy 3: Product Differentiation

"Don't knock your competitors. A little competition is a good thing, and severe competition is a blessing.
Thank God for the competition."
~ Jacob Kindleberger

The goal of product differentiation is to distinguish your product from other products in the marketplace. Differentiation is more than being different; it is creating more value, utility, and satisfaction for customers. For small farmers, product differentiation provides a competitive advantage, especially when competing with mega-corporations.

Many people are skeptical of large corporations. Treat this skepticism as a marketing opportunity. As a small farmer, you can invite people into your world and get them involved with your operation. Having people touch plants or interact with animals allows people to experience the masterpiece that is your farm. This interaction is a unique experience that increases trust while building customer loyalty; it also differentiates your product.

Choose words wisely. Words are free. This makes word choice and usage the most economical source of differentiation. Words used to describe processes and products are the foundation of the small farm and mega-corporation differentiation. Words are powerful; words first shape your perception of your farm and its products. You then share this perception with other people as you interact with them.

People will talk about your products by comparing them to similar products. These comparisons define your products in terms of other people's products. Your job is to manage this process. Talk about your products in a way that eliminates the commoditization of your work. Focus on product uniqueness, farm purpose, and the overall superiority of your products.

Here is a list of words to describe your farm:
- Agrarian
- Artisan
- Bio-diversity
- Cage-free
- Chemical-free
- Clean
- Community
- Cultivate
- Environmental
- Ethical
- Family
- Farm to Table
- Free Range
- Fresh
- Grass-fed
- Healing
- Healthier
- Heirloom
- Heritage
- Holistic
- Husbandry
- Local
- Mission
- Natural
- Non-GMO
- Pasture
- Passion
- Polyculture
- Raised in dirt
- Regenerative

- Rejuvenate
- Restorative farming
- Salad bar
- Self-sustaining
- Soil not dirt
- Sustainable
- Systems
- Traditionally Raised

Here is a list of words to describe the competition:

- Big-Ag
- Biologically engineered
- Cancer-causing
- Chemical
- Chemically engineered
- Conventionally raised
- Corporate
- Dumbed down
- Exploitation
- Faceless
- Factory Farm
- Feedlot
- Fillers
- GMO
- Greedy
- Herbicides
- homogeneous
- Industrial AG
- Manipulative
- Mass-produced
- Monoculture
- Pesticides
- Profit-driven not quality driven
- Scientifically designed
- Scientifically engineered
- Suicide seeds
- Standardization
- Terminator seeds

In addition to word choice, differentiation includes new products, services, practices, or processes. New products and services are what most people think of when they think of differentiation.

New, value-added products come with startup costs; however, they can provide year-round cash flow and increased profits. For small farms, this typically involves raising heirloom produce, heritage animals, and creating value-added products.

Many people want to buy from small farms because of farm practices or processes. Sharing your methods and procedures not only differentiates your product, but it increases customer confidence in your product. This means even if you are growing the exact same tomato as the local supermarket, people will pay a premium just because they know you and your practices.

Farm practices and processes are central to people who care about the environment. This is a natural source of differentiation that is often overlooked.

To differentiate your farm, answer the following four questions:

1. What are three to five things that make your farm operation unique?

_____

_____

_____

_____

2. What processes do you use to raise your products?

_____

_____

_____

_____

3. What makes your choice of product unique? For example, do you grow heirlooms? Are your animals registered or a heritage breed?

_____

_____

_____

_____

4. How are you going to talk about your products? What words and phrases are you going to use to describe your farm products?

_____

_____

_____

_____

Conclusion

Small farmers play a vital role in local economic development, caring for the environment, and sustaining communities. This makes small farm products more valuable than ordinary, run of the mill commodities.

Differentiation can be as simple as using different words to describe farm products, processes, and operations or as complex as developing value-added products. Either way, it is crucial to advocate your products as superior to similar products in the commodity market.

Small Farm Advertising Strategy 4: Express Value

*"It's easier to explain price once than to apologize for quality forever." ~ **Zig Ziglar***

Price is the sum of all your farm's activities. Pricing is the most critical accounting activity, as well as one of the most important marketing activities for the success of your farm. It is tempting to want to compete on price, but this puts you into direct competition with places such as Walmart, Kroger, and Costco – while also limiting your income.

Price reflects the value a customer places on a product and not the cost to produce the item. As a farmer, you need to focus on farm products or services that have economic value. Do not be afraid to charge for those products. There are limits to what you can charge, but it is best to push those limits.

To push limits, focus on quality products, professional packaging, and relationship building. As a rule of thumb, I price according to upscale sellers. I do this because someone somewhere is willing to pay this price. I also believe my product is just as good as what the high-end places are charging. Higher rates also provide negotiating room - it is always easier to lower prices than to raise prices.

Here is a worksheet that will help determine your prices. To complete this worksheet, visit several places and record the prices. Make a note of the lowest and highest prices.

Visit 3 – 5 locations for each row.

Location	Low	High	Average
Grocery Store			
Internet			
Road Side Stand			
Farmers Market			
Other?			
Average			

Based on this I should charge _____.

Based on what I charge, I should make _____ profit per unit and _____ profit per season/year.

The market will ultimately determine the price if you cannot make a profit at those prices, select products that are more profitable. I do grow a few products that are not profitable, but it is because I like to produce these items. They are mainly for my consumption and enjoyment. Growing unique items is not always profitable, but they do make great conversation starters. For the buyers who find you with that product, it creates instant loyalty.

I do not use input costs when calculating the price. Customers do not care what it costs to produce an item; they only care about the purchase price. This advice goes counter to what many other people recommend. As a believer in free markets, I believe customer demand determines the price.

Conclusion

The market determines the price. If you cannot make a profit at the market, consider a different market or a different product. There are typically many markets you could choose to be a part of! Lastly, there is nothing wrong with slightly higher than average prices. As a matter of fact, many people will gladly pay higher prices because they view it as a sign of quality.

Small Farm Advertising Strategy 5: Effective Small Farm Phone Skills

"One of the most powerful scientific tools ever invented is the telephone." ~ *John C. Mather*

The phone is typically the first human interaction new customers have with a farm. This initial conservation is the first step in building a long-term relationship. Since phones have become an extension of us and are generally always with us, it is essential to remember how critical professionalism is in the first interaction. Here are eleven best practices to ensure your farm's first impression is positive.

Best Practices for Small Farms: Phone Skills

Best Practice 1: Answer Promptly. The rule of thumb is to answer the phone within three rings, if possible. A prompt answer shows the caller; they are valued. This promptness creates a favorable first impression of your farm.

Best Practice 2: Use the Three-Part Greet. Use a three-part greeting Such as good morning/afternoon/evening thanks for calling (your farm name) this is (your name) how may I help you? This goal is to let the person know you are glad they are calling, and you are eager to help.

If your cell phone is your business phone, it is your business phone first and your personal phone second. Your mom won't mind a formal greeting, but an informal greeting will deter a first-time customer.

Best Practice 3: Smile. Smiling people are more enthusiastic, friendly, and inviting. People will hear your smile, and this sets the tone for a more productive conversation. Work to be sincerely glad someone called your farm – even if you were in the field mending fences, and the call was an interruption.

Best Practice 4: Name Usage. Friends call each other by their name. You want to treat customers like friends and make them feel like you care. When using a person's name, it shows you care while reducing any tension that may be present. Using a person's name is evidence you care about them on a personal level.

I know when I use a person's name, it relaxes me. It creates conservation. When one person relaxes, it encourages the other person to relax, and before you know it, two people are having a real, meaningful conversation.

Best Practice 5: Feedback Signals. By paraphrasing, repeating, and asking questions, you are letting the other person know that you care and comprehend the conversation. This creates a feedback loop that keeps meaning from being lost while moving the conversation forward.

Best Practice 6: Understand their Purpose. Is the person looking for directions? Looking to buy or seeking information? Take notes as the person is talking. This guides the conversation and questions while providing a record for later if needed.

Best Practice 7: Be Useful. The phone call is a customer service situation; therefore, focus on customer needs. If you cannot help this customer, get them help even if it means sending them to a competitor. I have a neighbor who sells the same produce I do. He never refers people to me, but I will refer people to him. I do this because I am building goodwill with customers. I also do this because I believe in any business you can never go wrong by doing whatever is best for the customer.

Best Practice 8: Recap. When ending the conversation, recap the purpose and action taken. This ensures the customer is happy, and happy customers are the best customers. This also saves time by eliminating a future phone call.

Best Practice 9: Thank them. Let the caller know you appreciate the call and remind them to call you again if a need arises. Always remember to encourage them to visit your website or social media pages for additional information.

Best Practice 10. Follow up as needed. You will not always be able to take care of the current need. As a business owner, it is your responsibility to take care of the follow-up. For example, if you sell produce and people are calling about tomatoes, and you are currently out, call those people back as soon as you have tomatoes.

Most people will not follow up. By following up, you are strengthening the bond between you and your customer. Following up is vital because it can increase future sales, remind the customer that you care, remind the customer of your products, and create a positive feedback loop around your business.

The best follow-up is always a phone call, but an email, text, or social media messages may work just fine. When in doubt on how to follow up with the customer, ask how they would like to be contacted in the future.

Best Practice 11. Voicemail. Most farms are small operations with the owners doing the bulk of the work. Even in the cell phone era, taking phone calls while driving a tractor, picking produce, or pulling weeds is not always practical. Most customers will understand this.

A common mistake is to think voicemail is just a tool for recording messages. Voicemail can do much more than that. Voicemail can extend your brand, promote products, and keep people up to date with information.

A correctly set up phone system eliminates unnecessary phone calls. Setting up your inbound phone calls, so people have an option to hear what products are available, hours, web address or other routine questions can save you and your customer time. It also adds to the professional image of your farm.

Voicemail is also an excellent opportunity for humor and for personalizing your farm and brand. For example, *"Thanks, for calling Ozark Family Farm. We love to talk to you, but we are busy chasing chickens/cows/pigs. Please leave a message with your name and number, and we will be glad to call you back as soon as we round these critters up. Make sure you visit our website ozarkfamilyfarm.com where you can find out more about us."* Humor goes a long when establishing a brand. It makes you approachable and real. People prefer doing business with real people, and customers will appreciate the attempt.

Conclusion

Even in the age of texts, emails, and social media, the phone is as essential as ever. Phone calls are connections with people interested in your farm; treat them as necessary. Remember, a phone call is not a distraction, but an opportunity to connect with another person.

Small Farm Advertising Strategy 6: Communicate Clearly, Concisely, and Correctly.

"You can have brilliant ideas, but if you can't get them across, your ideas won't get you anywhere." ~ **Lee Iacocca**

Effective communication is paramount. The purpose of communication is to create and share meaning. Communication is everything; it sculpts perception, binds relationships, and guides all human interactions. Compelling marketing is nothing more than excellent communication. This process does not just happen. It is the result of purposeful, intentional, and organized effort.

This is a marketing book; therefore, the communication discussion will be limited to interpersonal and written communication. The first section of this chapter will discuss thirteen best interpersonal communication practices, and the second section will discuss eleven best-written communication practices.

Use these best practices to manage your communication processes. Proper use of these practices will attract new customers and strengthen existing relationships.

Best Practices for Small Farms: Interpersonal Communication

Best Practice 1: Intentionality. Intent and purpose guide and give meaning to interactions. Each time we interact with another person, we either strengthen or weaken that relationship.

Intentional communication requires deliberate thought. This diligence emphasizes the importance of developing a long-lasting, meaningful relationship. If communication is not attentive, it becomes haphazard, leaving meaning and relationship-building to chance.

Best Practice 2. Stay Focused. Customers are looking for reasons to buy or not to buy from you. Customers are always judging. Pay attention to what you say and how you say it. Keep comments professional, polite, and positive. Speaking optimistically about things, people, and situations is always good business.

Best Practice 3: Be Conversational. Too often, people are self-absorbed in conversations. The best way to be conversational and engaging is to talk about what interests other people. Discovering and being concerned with the needs and interests of other people allows you to dig deeper into customer needs, and this becomes the foundation of a steady relationship.

The best communication is symmetrical. Listening to your customers serves two purposes. First, it lets your customers know you care. Second, it helps to explore their needs and wants. This insight guides new product and service development, making your farm more attractive, profitable, and sustainable.

Best Practice 4: Think like a Customer. People crave understanding. When you think like a customer, you are putting yourself in their situation, and as a result, you can make better customer service decisions. Taking care and relating to customers is always a good business practice.

Best Practice 5: Be a Translator. Your customer is not going to comprehend farm or agricultural jargon. One of the roles of being an excellent communicator is translating the language of farming into customer language. Phrase words and symbols in a way that makes it easy for your customers to understand.

Best Practice 6: Ownership. Customers should never initiate the conversation. It is your farm and your responsibility to ensure your farm's communication is effective. Take the initiative when starting conservations.

At every farmers market, farm store, or roadside stand, there are *chair sitters* and *standers*. The *chair sitters* wait for a customer to say something while they play on their phones. The *standers* are ready to start conversations with anyone who walks by.

The standers always sell more. The standers take ownership of the communication process. The most crucial step in taking ownership is speaking first. This initial greeting needs to be noncommittal, open, and friendly.

Best Practice 7: Listening. Do you just hear or understand what people say? Hearing is natural and passive, whereas listening requires attention, feedback, and being actively engaged in the conversation.

Listening is one of the most essential relationship-building strategies. Listening shows caring and concern. Bryant McGill said it this way, *"One of the sincerest forms of respect is actually listening to what another has to say."*

Best Practice 8: Clarification by Repetition. An effective way to ensure others understand exactly what you are communicating is to ask them to repeat their interpretation of the message. This creates a feedback loop where you can correct any miscommunication or misunderstandings.

Best Practice 9: Caring. To be a clear and effective communicator, recognize the message is not just about you, your desires, or completing a transaction. It is about the customer. In today's high tech and disconnected world, caring about another person provides a much-needed human connection.

Best Practice 10: Nonverbal. People cannot hear your words over your actions. When talking with someone, make eye contact, nod your head, and be interested. By checking your phone, looking way, or crossing your arms, you are shutting down effective communication by telling people they are not valuable.

Best Practice 11: Relational. You are building a relationship with your customers. Focus communication on building a relationship and not merely reacting to another person.

Best Practice 12: Conviction. The best-selling tool is a steadfast conviction in your product. The best way to have confidence in your product is to focus on quality. Where quality is the mantra confidence is a byproduct. Customers recognize and reward excellence with loyalty, willingness to pay higher prices, and positive word of mouth advertising.

Best Practice 13: Authenticity. Be a real standout in a fake world. There is only one you. Be your best while pursuing your passion and stand firm on your beliefs. People will respect this trait, and you will develop a profitable business.

Best Practices for Small Farms: Written Communication

Best Practice 1: Purpose. Are you selling? Are you telling? Are you explaining? Are you informing? As with verbal communication, your writing needs a purpose. This purpose guides words and makes reading marketing materials more attractive.

Best Practice 2: Medium Aware. Are you sending a letter or email? Are you writing an article or blog post? Are you drafting a brochure or flyer? Are you designing a sign? Each medium has its own nuances, rules, and expectations: know them.

Best Practice 3: Audience Aware. Who is your audience? Is it a new customer? Is it an old customer with an established relationship? Is it other farmers? Who are the members of the group that you are writing for? The writing and marketing materials must appeal to their interests.

Best Practice 4: Simple and Direct. Candid communication is the best communication. People are overwhelmed with messages today, many of which are convoluted. A simple and direct message is always the most effective.

Best Practice 5: Active Voice. Using the active voice makes your writing concise and efficient by creating a smoother narrative. This writing is easier to understand, edit, and more engaging.

Best Practice 6: Visual Appeal. Writing needs to be attractive. Proper formatting is essential for business writing and is vital for marketing. When written communication looks pleasing to the eye, it is easier to read and recall.

Best Practice 7: Bullet Points. Bullet points direct the reader's attention towards the main points. Bullet points are mini-headlines highlighting important information. Many people will only read the bullet points while other people will start with bullet points to determine if they want to keep reading.

Best Practice 8: Images. Pictures are masterful attention getters. Images make marketing materials come to life. When advertising, stock pictures, or graphics are great tools that make your small farm look professional. Candid photos make a farm come to life and feel warm and inviting. Images convey your brand by giving the audience a clear visualization of your products.

Best Practice 9: Avoid Jargon. Use simple everyday language. Avoid specialized phrases that are only known to farmers. This is frustrating for people who are just trying to figure out what you sell and where the farm is located. If you use an acronym, take the time to define what it means for your reader.

Best Practice 10: Templates. There is no need to reinvent the wheel. The internet is an excellent source of templates, many of which are free or low cost. Templates are great time savers while providing a polished, professional image. You could use them for newsletters, advertising, one-pagers, or infographics.

Best Practice 11: Brand Building. Always focus on moving your brand forward. The most valuable asset of any business is its brand. Always include your farm's logo in all written communication - print or electronic media.

Conclusion

Effective communication drives sales and marketing. Focus on being a great communicator, and your business will grow. Communication is the medium that we use to share our passion, purpose, and practices. It allows us to share meaning, build relationships, and connect with others.

Small Farm Advertising Strategy 7: Selling Your Farm

"To be yourself in a world that is constantly trying to make you something else is the greatest accomplishment."
~ Ralph Waldo Emerson

External greatness comes from internal beliefs. Maxwell Maltz said, *"Your most important sale in life is to sell yourself to yourself."* If you do not believe in your farm's practices, products, processes, or the person running it, you will never be able to sell yourself or products to other people.

There is no substitute for a person's confidence in their product. Would you trust a doctor who does not believe in medicine? Would you take your rowdy puppy to a training class if the trainer didn't believe in the outcome?

Contrast this to people who believe in their work. For example, musicians who feel the music are better performers. Actors who become the character are more believable. Farmers who put beliefs into action are better stewards of the land and producers of better products.

Farming is a precarious pathway to financial success. Self-doubt makes that pathway impossible. Eliminate any self-doubt and replace it with self-efficacy. Replace negative thinking with positive thinking. Stop dwelling on why things will not work and develop reasons why they will work. Turn off talk radio, the news, and TV and turn on motivation, inspirational, and informational audio or video programs.

A small farm allows farmers to live and express their passion and purpose. You have an opportunity to live life on your terms. To aid on your journey, here are 12 best practices to follow.

Best Practices for Small Farms: Selling Your Farm

Best Practice 1: Be You. Farming gives me a sense of independence. If you are like me, you thrive on that sense of freedom. Do not sacrifice it by masquerading as someone else. The world is becoming more homogeneous and less intriguing by the minute. Resist it and fight back by being you. This counterattack makes you a leader as well as a fascinating human.

Local and regional flair are losing ground to corporate consistency. This makes people hungry for authenticity. Feed that hunger by being something real. Remember, authenticity is a competitive advantage that mega-corporations cannot copy.

In any business, real people making real connections is the best practice for long-term success. On this subject, Bruce Lee offers this advice, *"Always be yourself, express yourself, have faith in yourself, do not go out and look for a successful personality, and duplicate it."*

Best Practice 2: Trustworthiness. Customers are the core business relationship. Honest dealings with people are the only way to build credibility, loyalty, and brand awareness. People will find out quickly if you are dishonest.

There are many farmers (and people in general) who are shortsighted. They will take a dollar today while sacrificing a lifetime of future dollars from loyal customers. Do not be that person. Be the person building a business for all tomorrows.

Best Practice 3: Be Passionate. Passion creates energy. Sharing this energy galvanizes people. Sharing this energy involves answering two questions:
- Why do you farm? Do not give a superficial answer. Answer this question on a deep emotional and spiritual level.
- What intrinsic rewards do you get from farming? Once again, this requires a deep and meaningful answer.

Always avoid answering these questions with the bland, boring, and wrong answer, "*to pay the bills.*" This commoditizes your products, minimizes your worth, insults passionate farmers, and drives customers away. This is the least motivating and inspiring response possible. If this is your real answer, rethink your career choices. Your answer should speak from your heart and soul.

Best Practice 4: Be a Guru. This requires learning your craft. Read books, attend workshops, listen to podcasts, and talk with farmers. The more fluent you are with farm practices, products, and trends, the higher your credibility. Most importantly, do not pretend; admitting shortcomings boosts credibility while pretending weakens it.

Learning must be intentional. Focus your learning on knowledge and wisdom. Abigail Adams said, *"Learning is not attained by chance, it must be sought for with ardor and diligence."* It is required to be diligent and deliberate when learning; if you do this, learning will provide a lifetime of rewards.

Best Practice 5: Stay Humble. Humble people are approachable and likable. Share failures and setbacks with others. People like stories; therefore, share your stories of what worked and what did not work.

Small farm success depends on building relationships. The more you talk and self-disclose, the more kinship will be present in the relationship with your customers. Self-disclosure is a humbling experience. Dwyane Johnson said, *"Be humble. Be hungry. And always be the hardest worker in the room."* Advice that is very applicable to farming.

Best Practice 6: Accessibility. Let people into your world. This is the first step in community building. Customers are a valuable part of your farm community. Make it a point to connect with the people making your farm possible.

Best Practice 7: Be Valuable to Others. Help other people get what they want. Zig Ziglar always said, *"You can get what you want if you help enough other people get what they want."* Good business is about helping people get what they want. As a small farmer, you do this by assisting people in getting healthy and delicious farm-fresh food.

Best Practice 8: Social Media Aware. Social media allows you to build a fan base that can turn mouse clicks into dollars. In today's world, using social media is essential. Social media allows communication directly with customers in a very dynamic way.

Social media is a great way to move product, connect with people, and build a business. I use social media to sell many products. Social media has allowed me to sell more products to more people allowing me to earn higher profits.

Social media needs managing. It is self-sabotaging not to use social media. It is incredible the number of small farms not using social media. As a matter of fact, many small farmers are afraid of social media. Today's customers desire to connect with their farmer; social media is a great tool to develop that bond.

Best Practice 9: Be the Message. Every word you say and every action you take sends a message. When you own a farm, people are judging your farm based on everything you say or do. It is important to remember you are always the official spokesperson of your farm.

Remember what Theodore Roosevelt said, *"Great thoughts speak only to the thoughtful mind, but great actions speak to all mankind."* Right words are essential, but action reveals actual values, beliefs, and purposes.

Best Practice 10: Be Brave. Do what others will not do; stand up for your farm's values. It seems many businesses are afraid to stand up for what is right. Stand out in the marketplace by standing up for your beliefs, values, and purpose.

If you make a mistake, admit it. Denying or avoiding responsibility is a sign of weakness. The easiest way to prevent a crisis management situation is to acknowledge the error, take responsibility, state what you are going to do differently in the future, and then move forward.

Best Practice 11: Follow Through. If you are going to follow, follow through. Follow through demonstrates integrity. Follow-through is a relationship strategy that cultivates commitment. Whether personal or professional, when a person follows through, they express caring and concern.

Best Practice 12: Believe in Potential. Belief in potential is more robust than expertise. Research indicates when judging others, people prefer the potential they see in the other person than that person's accomplishments. This is excellent news for starting farmers seeking to acquire customers. When you believe in your potential, others will believe in you.

Wilma Rudolph said it this way, *"Never underestimate the power of dreams and the influence of the human spirit. We are all the same in this notion: The potential for greatness lives within each of us."*

Conclusion

Sell yourself without selling yourself short. Have confidence in your farm's practices and products. This confidence creates customer excitement and engagement while building a thriving business.

As you sell yourself, focus on potential. Selling potential is a way to profit from self-belief and self-assurance. People admire rags to riches stories, and selling your potential creates a narrative outlining your future accomplishments. This allows customers to contribute to your farm story.

Small Farm Advertising Strategy 8: Tell Your Marketing Story

"Your brand is a story unfolding across all customer touchpoints." ~ **Jonah Sachs**

Marketing is storytelling. In business, if you do not control your story, other people will. Small farmers compete against big corporations who want people to think of small farms as dinky, know-nothing, subpar operations with a product that can't possibly measure up to the level of big-ag. As a small farmer, you must combat that message by letting people know the opposite is true. Many small farms experience success; the successful ones have a story to tell, and they consistently say it.

Corporations employ legions of marketing experts whose jobs are to create stories designed to convince people to do business with them instead of with you. These marketing experts are more concerned with gaining market share, profits, increasing stock price, and their next job or promotion.

Corporate marketing cares for their profit alone and not about customers, local communities, food systems, environmental issues, or the overall economy. The well being of rural America and the farming community is not even on their radar. Their sole concern is selling more stuff to people at higher prices. Sadly, these individuals have no attachment to land, animals, plants, or farm life. Their single attachment is with advertising, marketing, and public relations.

They seek to destroy small farms and producers by developing emotional stories and appeals void of reason and fact. People make purchasing decisions based on emotion and not reason or logic. Corporate marketers understand human emotions and intentionally exploit emotions, wants, and needs for corporate greed and gain.

Traditionally farmers have been a practical group of people. Reasonable people are more concerned about function than form. Sensible people do not strategize manipulation methods. They are busy working and getting ready for the next season. However, small farmers must develop their marketing skills, and, as a group, we need to understand direct marketing is just as important as seeds, livestock, fertilizer, rain, or any other farm input.

Successful small farming is the result of successful marketing. Haphazard marketing just happens, good marketing is easy, but great marketing requires a carefully constructed plan. When planning farm marketing, treat it as a never-ending story with your farm as a protagonist who champions environmental, health, and local issues for the benefit of customers and the community.

Create a courageous story. Courageous stories tell tales of struggle, valiance, and overcoming the odds. Building this theme into your core values and expressing it through your farm's vision and mission statement counters the damaging marketing messages from corporate America.

Compelling stories always include the protagonist, antagonist, and conflict. Expressing your farm's mission in Quixote fashion positions you and your farm as the protagonist in an epic struggle to save America from evil corporate forces. This narrative turns farm practices and processes into combative actions that disrupt the methods and procedures of corporate greed and manipulation.

At the risk of losing my MBA, I think it is entirely appropriate to demonize corporate America and greed as well as government regulations while championing small farms. I say this for three reasons.

First, the actions of corporations and the government facilitate economic decline in rural America. Corporations exploit small communities and drain them of resources. When a large box store enters a small market, the profit travels thousands of miles away to its headquarters. From there, it may move out of the country through transfer mispricing or price manipulation as a tax evasion strategy.

Second, farming regulations favor Big-Ag and not small farmers. For example, I can no longer buy feed-grade antibiotics for my livestock without a prescription from a veterinarian. I am a small cattle producer in an area without a large animal vet. If I do get a vet, he or she travels over an hour to get here, if he or she can get here at all.

Granted, liquid antibiotics for shots are available at the feed store; however, rounding up and putting a sick bovine in a squeeze chute adds stress to an already ill animal. This animal is now a danger to itself and humans. This is why food-grade antibiotics were more economical and safe.

Contrast that to the feedlots who have veterinarian(s) on staff. They are easily able to get scripts, food-grade antibiotics, and a host of other things that are illegal for me to purchase. The stated goal of this regulation was to limit antibiotic use, but the practice is an increased burden on small producers. At the same time, the big boys are doing business as usual, without any real impact on the overall use of antibiotics in the food chain.

Many government regulations limit rural economic development in the name of public safety. For example, there are rules on meat processing, raw milk commerce, poultry raising, hog raising, and food processing. A few make sense, but many do not. Basing regulations on empirical data is excellent; however, it seems that protecting large industry guides the majority of farm or health regulations.

Finally, comparing and contrasting your small practices to that of Big-Ag allows people to see that group as the problem and you as the solution to the problem. This is very effective, given the following facts.

People have a distrust of corporate America. According to Gallup, only 25% of Americans trust big business. As more proof, Fast Company published an article entitled *Americans agree on something – they don't like big corporations,* and this article stated, *"Americans are down on corporations. Almost two-thirds (62%) distrust the Fortune 500, and nearly half (47%) say business behavior is headed in the wrong direction, according to a new poll."*

Market research and anecdotal observations confirm that trust in big business and government is falling. For small farms, this is a huge marketing opportunity. Small farmers can do something that big business cannot: build personal relationships with customers.

People buy on emotions. Small farmers who put passion in front of profits are more alluring than faceless corporations who only care about profit. Telling your story means sharing your passion, purpose, and principles. As you tell your story, it is okay to be hokey, eccentric, or odd. Many people will find those quirks attractive and authentic.

Best Practices for Small Farms: Marketing Stories

Best Practice 1: Express Purpose. The majority of people passively pay attention to most advertising. Research by the American Marketing Association states that when an audience knows the purpose of an ad, it makes it more effective. The same body of research indicates that single and straightforward messages are the most powerful messages when measured in terms of recall.

Best Practice 2: Use the active voice. Active voice is specific, direct, and attention-getting. With an active voice, the subject (your farm) is performing an action. For marketing purposes, this action is heroically fighting industrial agriculture, corporate manipulation, and the ever-increasing homogeneous commodity-driven food system that is the root cause of the obesity epidemic and decay of rural economies.

Active voice makes it clear who is doing what and why. Marketing through storytelling defines the "why" using grandiose language. Big and bold claims, statements, and carefully created narratives attract supporters.

Marketing professionals understand that people will spend more money on the "why" (your mission) than the "what" (your product). Small farmers need to use this information and focus on the explanation of "why" if they are going to turn commodity farm products into extraordinary tools for social justice and environmental retribution.

Best Practice 3: Use imagery. Visual appeal is essential. With farm or food products, people buy with their eyes before their stomachs. Proper graphics allow people to visualize the desired outcome of using your product. The right layout makes marketing materials more comfortable to read while communicating professionalism.

Best Practice 4: Use specific nouns. Using concrete terms gives customers a tangible visualization. Specific words create vibrant and appealing marketing materials.

Specific nouns for farm marketing mean using breed and variety names of animals and plants instead of broad, generic names. These specifics can include farm practices, location, or origin. Here are a few examples:

Generic Noun	Specific Noun
Chicken	Pasture-raised chicken Farm-raised chicken Rocky mountain hens Heritage breed Rhode Island Red, Breese, or other breeds
Beef	Angus, Longhorn, Wagyu, or any specific breed Heritage beef Ozark raised beef Pasture-raised Farm-raised Grass-fed Spring watered
Eggplant	Japanese White Egg Cookstown Orange Heirloom Soil raised Naturally raised Farm fresh
Tomato	Heirloom Brandywine Cherokee Purple Vine-ripened Farmer approved Old fashioned

I am in the cattle business. Weekly I hear from other cattlemen how the Angus "people" did a great job hoodwinking people into believing black cows are the best cows. I usually do not argue and just nod in agreement.

I happen to disagree that Angus is the best cow because I raise the best cows: Wagyu. I do acknowledge the Angus association did a great job using specific nouns and storytelling to create a great story and to differentiate their product.

Best Practice 5: Use simple language. Avoid farm jargon. People need to understand the language used in your advertising; it should be short and straightforward.

The average American reading level is the 7th or 8th-grade level, and this is the recommended level for instructional manuals and medical instructions. Most mass-market fiction books are written on a 5th to 6th-grade level because most people feel comfortable reading below their reading level.

The purpose of marketing material is to get people to read something and take action and not to increase the nation's literacy level. Simple language and simple sentences are best for marketing messages.

Best Practice 6: Simple Sentences and Fragments.
Writing marketing materials is not about impressing people with your extensive vocabulary and your thesaurus use. The goal of marketing is to get the point across and to get people to buy something or to take action, such as visiting your farm's website or following your farm's social media profile.

Best Practice 7: Focus on Branding. Controlling the story means controlling your branding story. An early chapter of this book is on branding; review that section as branding is everything in business as well as the driving force of your farm's story.

Best Practice 8: Conversational Dialogue. Convincing people require *"talking with"* them instead of *"talking to"* them. Marketing is about persuasion; it is easier to convince people to buy your farm's products through conversations than a factual lecture.

Best Practice 9: Be Original. Originality is a theme throughout this book because it allows you to separate yourself from the competition. Competitors can duplicate all your products and services, but you are non-replicable. At the same time, you get more new original ideas by growing as a person. You should always be learning and growing. Bernard Meltzer said it this way, *"If you want to be original, just try being yourself, because God has never made two people exactly alike."*

Best Practice 10: Concise Messaging. If you are advertising on TV or radio, you have just 30 seconds to grab people's attention and to express your point. On social media, people will only watch videos for a minute or two. If you are creating text for websites or print, people will not read essays or long narratives. If you are developing a flyer or brochure, people want simple bullet points with pictures.

Conclusion

Telling your marketing story is essential. Your marketing theme compares and contrasts your farm's practices with that of Big-Ag and corporate America. When done correctly, marketing positions a farm as the best alternative to the dangers of mega-corporations who do not care about their customers or the environment.

Small Farm Advertising Strategy 10: Professional Signage

"A business with no sign is a sign of no business."
~ Old Saying

Small farms often overlook the importance of attractive signage. Do not make that mistake. For a small farm, a professional sign communicates that you are legitimate, sincere, and dependable. As a matter of fact, market research from FedEx found that 80% of new customers choose to visit a new store because of the attractiveness of its sign.

Signs say you are a real business providing high-quality products. A sign is an invitation for customers to stop in, visit you, and buy something. Farm signs are some of the most efficient and cost-effective forms of marketing. Good signs are an investment that provides the following three benefits.

1. Increasing brand exposure. Farm signage tells customers that you are serious about farming. A sign builds a farm's brand exposure while inviting new customers to get to know you.

2. Cost-effective. Good quality signs last. The startup costs may be high, but once installed, a sign works 24 hours a day, 7 days a week. If the start-up costs are an issue, a simple printed sign can go a long way.

3. Year-round advertising. While you may not sell farm products year-round, a sign reminds people you will be there next season.

Eleven Best Sign Practices for Small Farms

Best Practice 1: Concise Text. The best signs communicate a farm's brand in just a few words. A general rule is to use 10 words or less; therefore, make every word count.

Best Practice 2: Crucial Communication. A farm's sign must express precisely what customers need to know before visiting the farm. A farm's sign needs the following information:

- Farm name with logo.
- Phone number with area code
- Website
- Slogan/moto
- Call to action
- Hours/days of operation

Best Practice 3: Text Appeal. Too much text conceals the message; use just enough words, so people know that you are a farm open for business.

Best Practice 4: Font Type. Fonts must be consistent. It is vital to use the same font from your logo in your signage. This font needs to be easily readable from a distance. The seven most common sign fonts are Arial, Helvetica, Futura, Garamond, Bodoni, Trajan, and Frutiger. You are not limited to these fonts; just make sure whatever font you use is easily readable (and not Comic Sans!).

Font size is essential. Below is a standard visibility chart showing font size in inches with viewing distance in feet.

Letter Visibility Chart

Letter Size/Height in inches	Viewing Distance if feet
4	100
10	250
16	360
33	500
43	1,000
57	1329 (1/4 mile)

Best Practice 5: Color Contrast. The colors you select should be consistent with your branding efforts and easy to read. The font and background must have contrasting colors. Here is a chart that will help you:

Best Color Combinations	
Letters	**Background**
White	Black
Yellow	Black
Orange	Black
Black	White
Blue	White
Green	White
Red	White
White	Red
White	Orange
Black	Yellow
White	Blue

Best Practice 6: Focal Point. A farm's sign is a focal point. First, a sign must convey the most essential information in a way that grabs attention. Second, the sign should be close to the entry point or another point of interest.

Best Practice 7: Limit Graphics. With outdoor signs, the fewer the graphics, the better. Use the farm's logo while keeping other graphics purposeful. It is better to leave off other graphics as it clutters the sign and distracts from the message. Make sure your graphics compliment your brand and sign. If they don't, you are better off without them.

Best Practice 8: Capitalization. Signs using all capital leaders are more challenging to read. Use a suitable mix of uppercase and lowercase letters. All caps are akin to yelling, and no one likes to be YELLED at.

Best Practice 9: Clean, Clear View. Signs need a clear line of sight for customers. The farm sign may be the only impression people have of your farm. Keep the sign neat, clean, and well lit. Lastly, keep the trash picked up and the area around the sign well maintained.

Best Practice 10: Lighting. Signs should be readable at night. Most signs have a spotlight illuminating the sign, but some signs are backlit. A light shining brightly on a sign is a great way to make a farm shine.

There are LCD signs that can make farms look high-tech. These are usually quite expensive and may not fit the farm's brand. I mention them because they are easy to change and offer other benefits.

Best Practice 11: Golden Ratio. The Golden Ratio built the greatest works of art as well as the most recognizable architecture designs throughout human history. Here is a template of what it looks like:

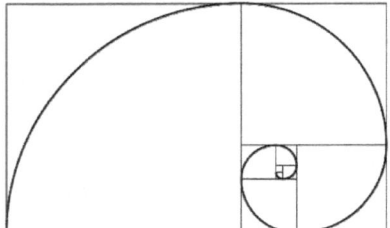 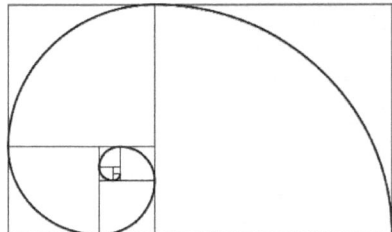

Arrange the text and graphics on your farm's sign according to the Golden Ratio. Most sign companies understand this concept; therefore, be sure to tell them that you want your sign designed according to the Golden Ratio. **If they have never heard of the Golden Ratio, use a different sign company.**

Conclusion

A sign is an investment, but it doesn't need to be cost-prohibitive. Proper signage builds business and offers 24/7 marketing. It is more than a cliché to say a company without a sign is a sign of no business. Small farm profitability means running the small farm as a professional business, and a good quality sign signals professionalism.

Small Farm Advertising Strategy 11: Provide Excellent Customer Service

"Excellent customer service is the number one job in any company! It is the company's personality and the reason customers come back. Without customers, there is no company."
~ Connie Elder

Customers are the lifeblood of small farms. Customers bring money into the farm enterprise. This money allows farmers to farm, pay bills, support families, and grow. Successful small farms focus on customers and make farm decisions, including what products to raise, based on customer needs and wants. I believe the single best thing a small farm can do for its long-term success is taking care of customers.

I often see social media memes or messages that say, "Eaten today? Thank a farmer." The meme should read, "If you farmed today, thank a customer." The idea that a customer should thank a supplier is misdirected.

Farming is the only industry I am aware of that thinks this way. Imagine going to a fast-food restaurant and thanking the owner for selling you a milkshake or buying a new vehicle and thanking the CEO for building that car. Every industry but farming seems to understand the importance of customers.

My neighbors and many farmers criticize me for saying customers are not dependent upon farmers. That is fine, and they are free to make business decisions based on that belief.

If farmers disappeared, people would adapt. Humans always have and will meet challenges and environmental changes. The reason we live in this modern human world is as a species we excel at adapting. For the bulk of human existence, people raised or gathered their own food, and people could do it again if they needed to.

Farmers are not going to suddenly vanish. Yes, small farms are declining, and cultivated land is decreasing in terms of acreage, but the overall output of food is increasing. Besides, the number of people interested in locally sourced food is growing as well as the number of people involved in homesteading. Lastly, the demand for safe, delicious, and healthy food is at an all-time high.

Whenever there is a demand for a product or service, someone in the economy will meet that demand. There will always be people willing to farm and eager to replace those people who are leaving farming. How do I know people are keen to farm? I know because you are reading this book. **It is just plain silly to make a business decision based on a hypothetical situation with no chance of happening.**

Third, there are small and large farmers filing bankruptcy this year. If farmers, large or small, did not need customers, why are they going out of business? Obviously, farmers need money. However, the phrase, "Thank a Farmer..." implies that farmers do not need customers (or money) and that farmers are working out of a sense of altruistic duty.

Empirical evidence is overwhelming that farmers need people to buy their products. Farmers need cash more than they need silos full of grain, barns full of hay and pastures full of livestock. Therefore, do not take customers for granted. When a customer supports your farm, they are allowing you to live your dream; be appreciative of that support.

Eight Best Customer Service Practices for Small Farms

Best Practice 1: Quality Products. The best way to stand behind your product is to offer quality products. When you bring quality to the marketplace, customers will be happy. Providing a quality product in a friendly manner separates your farm from farms expecting people to thank them for growing something as well as separating you from big box stores that don't emphasize customer contact.

When I am at a farmers market, and someone complains about a previous purchase I immediately offer a replacement or refund. I have never asked for a receipt or proof that they made the purchase; I just make it right.

Some vendors are critical of that approach. They claim I am naïve, and I am letting people take advantage of me. They also say this forces them to also give refunds. Other vendors praise my approach and say it is good for them and the market when all vendors stand behind their products. I do it because that is how I want to be treated and how much I believe in my product.

Best Practice 2: Reward Repeat Purchases. This is quite easy and simple. Create a punch card. Whenever someone purchases an item, punch the card. When the card is complete, offer a discount, free product, or farm swag (t-shirt or hat with your farm name/logo). Make it something worthwhile; otherwise, it will just be insulting to your customer and counterproductive to your marketing efforts.

Best Practice 3: Use Names. This could be the most effective customer service and sales strategy of all time. Learning people's names is the most personal connection you can make. Using a person's name connects you and your farm with that person's world and identity. Lastly, it makes them feel as if you know each other.

People prefer doing business with a friend instead of doing business with a stranger. This creates a powerful contrast with major retailers with high staff turnover, and as a result, are unable and unwilling to meet their customers on such a personal level. This is a concrete example of a compelling differentiation and relationship strategy you have that large businesses do not have.

Best Practice 4: Thank You Cards. Collect people's names and information by using a fishbowl for business cards or have people sign up for a mailing list. Harvest these names and send a brief handwritten note thanking them for their purchase and support of small farms. This is a quick and easy gesture that pays dividends.

Thank you notes are quickly becoming a lost art, and by sending thank you letters, you are building goodwill with customers and adding a little something extra to the relationship that most other people will neglect.

Best Practice 5: Giveaways. Give people a little extra. An extra cucumber, tomato, onion, or garlic clove is not going to hurt your bottom line. Sometimes a customer may just want one of something like an onion, and if they have already spent a significant amount of money with you, just give it to them. Giving something extra is more impactful for your farm's future than an extra dollar.

This will pay dividends because it creates loyal customers. I know a blueberry grower who raises cut flowers that he gives away. As he gives these flowers away, most people will buy at least one box of blueberries. If they do not buy anything, they tell friends or other people about the blueberry man giving away flowers. This grower always sells out and goes home before me.

Best Practice 6: Customer Profiles. Create a list or database of your best customers and send birthday or holiday cards. These cards make a connection with your customers and allow you and your farm to celebrate their special days with them.

Social media makes this easy. Facebook sends notifications of your friend's birthdays. Use these notifications to wish that person a happy birthday or offer them a free product.

Best Practice 7: Be Friendly. This should be the most comfortable and most natural aspect of customer service. I am amazed at the number of small businesses that are not nice to their customers. They act as if their customers are some sort of adversary or interruption instead of the reason they are in business. When you treat customers like friends, they will become your friends and lifelong customers.

Best Practice 8: Discounts. There are benefits to moving lots of products. Selling out is always profitable and fun. Besides, if you are like most farms, you are not going to sell everything you grow; therefore, it is better to offer a discount than it is to throw more produce on the compost pile.

There is also the transactional cost to consider. Big sales reduce expenses, and it makes sense to share these savings with the customer. Sharing these savings encourages future big purchases, and big purchases are better than small purchases.

Conclusion

Farmers are dependent upon customers. If you are fortunate enough to farm full time, thank your customer. It is always a smart business decision to take care of customers. If you take care of the customer, the customer will take care of you. Small farmers need to be nurturing and managing customer service and treat it as a critical farm practice.

Small Farm PR:
8 Proven Strategies

*"A good PR story is infinitely more effective than
a front-page ad." ~ **Sir Richard Branson***

Public relations is about storytelling. In farming, as in
any industry, there are success stories or organizations that
seem unscathed by adversity. These "rock star" farms
know the importance of storytelling. Their day-to-day
farm operations are no different from your daily activities.
The **only** difference between these farmers and you are
their story-telling prowess.

These successful farmers create narratives to get people to
buy into why they are doing what they do and how they
do it. These farmers effectively use public relations to
develop, protect, and enhance their standing as industry
trailblazers and innovators. ***These farmers understand the
following eight benefits of public relations:***

1. Farm Branding. Public relations is not about selling a
product; it is about selling a farm's concept or mission.
Public relations build a farm's reputation by
communicating farm values, mission, and practices to the
public.

Reporting by Forbes claims 64% of people start a
relationship with a business because of the business'
values and reputation. Farm to table customers is a more
value-driven group than the broader population making a
farm's reputation critical.

2. Widespread Credibility. Public relations stories are more credible than traditional advertising. Many people look at news and media stories as a third-party endorsement.

The lifeblood of effective PR is having someone else report your story. Many people follow media personalities and believe they have relationships with these people. When these people talk positively about your farm, it becomes an endorsement.

3. Enlarged Customer Base. PR puts your farm's name in front of more people in more places. Even the smallest media outreach gives farm exposure to a new group of people. Farm growth requires additional customers, and effectively managing PR brings in these new customers.

4. Widened Network. Building a farm's network is essential. The more extensive the network, the more potential customers, suppliers, or other beneficial relationships can form. Increased networks offer more farm visibility while raising your personal and professional profile in the community. This expanded network is an excellent source of ideas for new products and services for a farm to offer.

5. Enhanced Farm Image. An early chapter in this book discusses becoming a brand and your farm's personality. A farm's personality drives its PR efforts. Consistent and frequent messaging is the most effective method to build a farm's image. Keeping a farm's personality consistent improves recall and creates a high-quality farm impression.

Ansel Adams said, *"There is nothing worse than a sharp image of a fuzzy concept."* For a farm's PR efforts, this means having a clear and focused visualization of its image. As you develop content, consider carefully the image being created.

6. Secured Future Business. Customers fade away for many reasons; some move, lose jobs, or will buy from a new or different farm. Effective PR is a way to build your customer pipeline before it runs dry. Remember the words of Benjamin Franklin, who said, *"Failing to prepare means you are planning to fail."* PR planning is just as important as planting crops, animal harvesting, or any other farm activity.

7. Greater Community. This is slightly different than building your network. A network is a loosely connected group of acquaintances, whereas a community is a close group of people you consider friends and family.

Farm community members are invested in the farm. Their investment could be in visits, purchases, or emotionally because of a combination of things. For example, our family once had an emotional investment in a local Christmas tree farm because it was our yearly tradition to go and buy a tree there.

The experience economy is growing, and farmers have a great opportunity in this competitive landscape. Big box retailers lack connection with customers due to their sheer size. As a small farmer, you can personally greet each person who visits the farm. This simple acknowledgment and human connection is a competitive advantage that large businesses cannot replicate.

8. Improved Profitability. Profits keep a farm open. Small farm profitability comes from building relationships. There is nothing wrong with striving for profitability. As a matter of fact, your farm's success is dependent upon profitability. Focusing on profitability builds a farm into something meaningful for you and the community.

Conclusion

Public relations is just as important as any other farm practice. Farmers as a group tend to be modest and have a hard time tooting their own horns. Do not frame this as bragging on yourself. Instead, you let people know that you are an alternative to Big-Ag, corporate America, or the current food system.

Embracing public relations allows small farmers to compete against the big players. Corporate retailers are using marketing, advertising, and public relations to increase their market share. Do not lose the opportunity to let people know how you are different and why it matters.

Small Farm PR Strategy 1: Write a press release

"If you don't tell your story, someone else will." ~ **PR axiom**

The press release is the foundational piece of any public relations program. A press release is a short story with a purpose. For a farm, this purpose is to inform people about new products, services, events, expansion, or other noteworthy announcements.

A press release keeps the media and their audience in touch with your farm. Local journalists, small farm publications, and bloggers are on the lookout for story ideas, and you are looking for increased exposure. This is an ideal match, but it is up to you to manage this relationship.

The more popular the media, the wider the reach; however, there is greater competition for that reach. When creating a press release, the goal is to make it captivating. The farm to table movement, locally grown, all-natural, or sustainable farm movements are trending. In short, this means local media people are actively searching for these types of stories. This is an advantage small farms have over other industries, businesses, or organizations.

When writing a press release, use a basic press release template available online. The form and layout are critical; however, content is king. When writing a press release, avoid the language of selling and use the language of telling. The best press releases reverberate as information sharing.

The absolute best practice for a press release is to sound as if you are telling a story. It should look like you have something urgent, engaging, and insightful to share with the world.

Best Practices for Small Farms: Press Releases

Best Practice 1: Seize Attention. Journalists, bloggers, or writers are busy professionals; the headline must quickly grab their attention. The headline of the press release is a gateway to the media; make it count. It must immediately grab the reader's attention, and it must draw them into your story.

Best Practice 2: Be Direct. Quickly getting to the point shows you care about the reporter's time. The first paragraph should be the meat and potatoes of the story. Think of it as a kind of thesis statement with the following paragraphs as sources of more in-depth information.

Best Practice 3: Numbers Count. A press release is a place for interesting facts, and numbers are always impressive. Use numbers as evidence of a story's importance. Quantifying an argument is the best way to make it believable, engaging, and relevant while building credibility.

Best Practice 4: Be Quotable. Here is an opportunity for your personality to shine. Quotes are the most essential part of the press release. The best practice for quotes is to use blocks, bullet points, or quotation marks. The best quotes are short, simple, and significant.

Best Practice 5: Be Visible. Include your contact information. This is a simple but overlooked item. Make it easy for the reader to find your name, your farm's name, website address, email address, social media info, and phone number with area code. Always include the farm's logo, phone number, and mission statement in the letterhead of any press release.

Best Practice 6: Well-timed. Make the announcement far enough in advance to give readers time to make plans. Also, different media organizations have different deadlines. As you build your media network, keep their deadlines in mind, and work with them. They are doing you a favor by telling your farm story their audience.

Best Practice 7: Visually Appealing. Formatting is important. The press release must be easy to read with good flow. Use bold headlines, bullet points, short paragraphs, and appropriate color, along with other formatting items that make it both readable and appealing.

A poorly formatted press release can make the most professionally managed farm look unprofessional. A professionally-formatted press release can make the most basic start-up appear established and reputable.

Best Practice 8: Short and Simple. The best press release is only one page, and never more than two pages. When writing press releases, keep them relevant and straightforward.

Best Practice 9: Express Personality. Keep the content fun. The best farms have personality, and that personality needs to shine through the press release. Think about the farm's values, beliefs, and principles and use the press release as a mechanism to convey those items.

Be Practice 10: Grammar Matters. Benjamin Franklin said, *"Either write something worth reading or do something worth writing about."* This is useful advice for a press release. Proofread the press release; let others proofread it as well. A single mistake can dissuade a reporter from taking you seriously. If something is worth writing about, it is worth writing about correctly. Paying attention to grammar reflects your professionalism while communicating the importance of your message.

Conclusion

Press releases keep your farm in the local news. As seasons change and new products become available, share this information through a press release. You are encouraging the media to share farm products, events, expansions, and other happenings with their readers. Even though some of this may be indirect exposure, it all adds up and keeps your farm's name in the spotlight.

Small Farm PR Strategy 2: Create a Press Kit

"Don't be afraid to toot your own horn." ~ **Emlyn Chand**

A press kit facilitates media exposure. A good working relationship with local media is vital for getting regular, positive press and for keeping a farm's name in the minds of potential customers. This requires effort and organization, and a press kit is the tool to organize that effort.

Jane Russell said, *"Publicity can be terrible. But only if you don't have any."* A press kit housed on your website makes the media's job easier. A quality press kit allows journalists to develop stories around your farm. This kit needs to include all the resources and content that a reporter, producer, or blogger needs to develop a story to share with their audience.

A press kit comes in a variety of forms: PowerPoint, Google Slides, Infographics, pdf, etc. The best kind is what works best for you while providing the necessary information for the reader.

Best Practices for Small Farms: Press Kits

Best Practice 1: Farm Background and History. The media needs to know who you are, what you do, and why you do it. This is typically the "about us" section found on many websites. This includes the basics: who, what, where, when, why, and how. It is best to keep this section concise and easily readable.

Best Practice 2: Your Bio. This is especially important for getting interviews, giving expert commentary, and speaking engagements. A bio is not a resume, but a brief narrative describing your journey to small farm leadership. You are not searching for a job, but you are searching for publicity. This narrative needs to include family, type of farm, awards, honors, and personal views that reflect the farm's mission, vision, and purpose. It's okay to be bold and confident. Put forth your best qualities in a sincere and meaningful manner without being pretentious. Most importantly, be you!

Writing bios in the third person is a matter of tradition and style. Writing in the third person makes the reader feel as if this is an endorsement of you instead of you bragging about yourself. Use facts to describe yourself and your accomplishments while avoiding first-person pronouns.

Best Practice 3: A Press Release Directory. A press release directory can be a page on your website that features some of the most newsworthy and inspiring press releases. When people see this on your website, it gives relevance and immediacy to your farm, your website, and your work. This list needs regular updating. A thriving farm is dynamic and inviting, and press releases serve as an invitation for people to learn more about the farm.

The press release heading should clearly describe its content. Saving press releases has benefits because an old press release may be of new interest to a new audience. Besides, it only takes a moment to add press releases to a website. This simple task builds credibility for the farm.

Best Practice 4: Information Sheets. Create informational sheets about your farm, products, and services. For example, if you host school field trips, you could have a field trip informational sheet with all the info a school or daycare would need in considering you as an option. Meat pricing information sheets are vital in communicating how much various purchases would be or explaining to people how to buy beef, chicken, or pork from you. Make sure all pertinent information is included, such as pricing, where to purchase, quantity discounts, and what products are in season.

Best Practice 5: Case Studies. Gather and create stories of people who have used your farm products. Did someone lose weight or lower their cholesterol after eating your veggies? If so, share this with the world. These referrals provide a reliable, firsthand account of the quality of your products. This turns customer comments and compliments into customer testimonials, which is always a convincing and valid form of promotion.

Case studies are very important for farmers who promote themselves as a mission or purpose-driven farm. For example, I follow a farm on social media who takes on Monsanto; currently, this farm has case studies about dicamba.

This farm gets lots of media coverage, and it is because of these case studies. Keep in mind that the media needs commentary on items like dicamba – this farm I follow becomes a default source for analysis because they follow this issue themselves and keep an active listing of news surrounding it on their website.

Best Practice 6: Prior Press Coverage. Unlike a press release directory, this is published articles from the media that highlight your farm. An old adage says, "press begets press." Prior press coverage is evidence of interest in your farm, and previous coverage makes media members more likely to recognize you as an industry leader.

A word of caution: most articles are copyrighted. It is safest to include the name of the outlet and a link to the original article on that media's website. This helps avoid any potential copyright infringement while saving space on your website and server.

Best Practice 7: Awards and Accolades. Awards and accolades build credibility while positioning your farm as a community leader. Update this section as needed. If you don't have any awards, consider a "customer comments" page – or, perhaps, "Fans of the Farm" for a catchier title.

Best Practice 8: Farm Images. Use high-quality professional artwork and logos. Graphics must be high-resolution for this section, and they must include the farm's logo, product images, and headshots of key members. These images add life to your story.

Visual content comprised of interesting imagery or videos is an essential element of PR. This may require an investment by using a commercial photographer or videographer. *When using professional photographers, make it clear you are buying the copyrights to the images or videos.* If the person you are talking with retains the copyright, find someone else who will transfer the copyrights to you.

Best Practice 9: Articles. Write articles for people to reference. This book contains a chapter on article writing. These articles are great for marketing, as well as becoming part of your press kit.

Best Practice 10: Contact Information. Make it easy for people to find you. Always include your email, phone number, and address in a visible place. You would be surprised at how frequently this step is overlooked!

Conclusion

A press kit makes it easy for media members to report on your farm. The easier you make it for people to report on your farm, the more press your farm will receive. The more positive press a small farm receives, the more customers and profits will find that farm.

Small Farm PR Strategy 3: Become an Expert

"We are all experts in our own little niches." ~ **Alex Trebek**

Becoming an expert is easy. Pick a subject and plunge yourself into it. You are obviously interested in farming. Therefore, pick an aspect of agriculture that most interests you and learn all you can about it. Developing this expertise enriches your farm's brand as well as your personal reputation.

Becoming an expert pays dividends. Ben Franklin said it this way, *"An investment in knowledge pays the best interest."* You will personally benefit from this knowledge. Being an expert helps you problem solve, train employees, educate customers, and expand your farm enterprise.

Being an expert helps with media attention. When local reporters need a farm-related expert, you can be that person. Each media appearance enhances your brand. Media appearances drive visitors to your website and garner new followers from social media.

Best Practices for Small Farms: Become an Expert

Best Practice 1: Task Mastery. Malcolm Gladwell, the author of *Outliers*, states it takes 10,000 hours of practice to master a skill. His book listed many examples, including Bill Gates, Thomas Edison, and Alexander Graham Bell. His next book could include you!

There is no substitute for time and energy. Becoming an expert requires dedication, discipline, and direction. To this end, Vince Lombardi offers the following advice, *"The price of success is hard work and dedication to the task at hand."* This quote confirms dedication is irreplaceable, and discipline is the cornerstone of dedication.

Discipline comes from the Latin word *disciplina*. When used as a noun, it refers to education, training, self-control, and determination in a field of study. Personal discipline allows for more than a cursory scan of a given topic. It enables you to become engrossed in a specific topic.

Direction determines depth. For this discussion, I am referring to the depth of knowledge. Experts have a deep understanding of subject matter, and you become an expert by diving deeply into the chosen subject matter. Plato says this about direction and education, *"The direction in which education starts a man will determine his future life."*

Experts have a sincere, genuine desire to move forward. An expert does a thing because doing that task is just what they do. I believe you farm because it is who you are, so, become a farm expert.

Best Practice 2: Nurture Your Network. Jim Rohn states, *"You are the average of the 5 people you spend the most time with."* Intentionally selecting a peer group of people with the knowledge and skills you are seeking puts that knowledge and expertise into reach.

Hanging out with people who have the skills you want to acquire will change how you think and approach farming. Deep and clear-thinking people bring diverse paradigms, expectations, and approaches to the conversation. Wisely choose the people you associate with, and it will benefit you, your customers, and your farm.

Best Practice 3: Mentor New Farmers. The most in-depth learning comes from teaching others. Teaching forces you to focus your attention on the details and nuances of farming. When people learn, they ask questions, and these questions create new perspectives while uncovering knowledge deficits.

Best Practice 4: Be Visionary. Visionaries expand possibilities by pushing boundaries. You should always be looking for ways to improve and solve problems. Visionaries are experts who create trends. This requires being solution-oriented rather than problem-oriented.

Visionaries question standard practices and modes of operations. This process of questioning and challenging the status quo allows for new product innovating and discovering new ways to serve customers. Your job as a visionary is to be future-minded by treating your farm as a hub of innovation. Remember, visionaries are experts with a sense of adventure.

Best Practice 5: Exhibit Expertise. Share what you know. Many groups are looking for lunch or keynote speakers. This is an excellent avenue for sharing your expertise while connecting with new customers. A little knowledge and confidence are all it takes to be a leader in the farm to table community.

Best Practice 6: Stay Current. Farming is changing; besides, the world is a dynamic place. The future of your farm depends on the mindfulness of these changes. So, be proactive and intentional when adapting to these changes. Analyze new trends and understand how these trends shape agriculture.

This does not mean you should jump on every new trend you come across; it also does not mean maintaining the status quo. It involves monitoring the economic environment and making changes to ensure the long-term viability of your farm.

This requires the foresight to see what technology and innovations can improve farm operations or better connect the farm with customers. Many farmers fight new trends, and as a result, many farmers will drown fighting that current just as people drown fighting rip tides. Do not be the farmer who drowns; be the farmer who sees currents and trends as a pathway to success.

Best Practice 7: Continuous Growth. Farmers grow many things, but many farmers do not grow themselves. The most important thing a farmer can grow is his or her mind. Farmers need to make time to read books, attend classes, listen to podcasts, and follow blogs. Learning something new is one thing you can do daily that will improve the future of your farm.

Best Practice 8: Earn Certificates. You can learn without getting a certificate; however, a certificate or degree is evidence that your expertise is legitimate. This is a third-party endorsement that you have attained a certain level of competence in a given area.

Notice, this says **earn** and not **get**. When earning a certificate, you focus on learning the material. People can get degrees or certificates by hoop-jumping, but hoop-jumping and actual learning are two different things. I tell my children that learning is more important than a grade. I would rather my children have a lower grade, but actually learn something than have my children **get** all As; learning is the goal.

Best Practice 9: Earn Awards. Earning awards communicates expertise and excellence. Winning honors and gaining recognition is always a great PR opportunity, and each award won is a reason to reach out and talk to the media. The award is not as important as the process. The process needs to build learning and expertise, and the award should represent that effort.

Best Practice 10: Be the Niche. Do not just have a niche – be the niche. Being the "niche" means you are the best in class. This is the result of a relentless focus on quality products while maintaining high customer service standards. Therefore, do not have a niche, but be the niche.

Conclusion

Being an expert is a matter of choice. Anyone willing to implement the 10,000-hour rule can become an expert. Being an expert is always a great business practice. Learning, honing, and expanding farming knowledge always pay dividends. I have never met a person who said, "My biggest problem is I learned too much."

Small Farm PR Strategy 4: Use a Professional Logo

"A poor logo doesn't mean a business will fail, and a good logo doesn't mean it will succeed - it just helps. Ultimately a good logo is something that people recognize instantly and relate to."
~ Matt Mickiewicz

Potential customers judge farms based on the quality of their logos, whether they know it or not. A farm's logo is its most important work of art. A logo is more than a visual representation of a farm's brand; it is a symbol of a farm's mission, values, beliefs, practices, processes, and products. A logo is the symbolic representation of all a farm stands for and hopes to become.

Symbols are powerful mediums of communication. Since the days of early history, people have used symbols to communicate deep meanings, convey messages, and express both ideas and values. A farm's logo is a significant symbol that needs careful development, defining, and designing.

A professional looking logo is an investment. There are websites and logo tools available to create a professional and appealing logo. If you have the right eye for detail and a flair for design, there is no reason that you could not use one of these tools. If you are mediocre or just bad with these tools, get professional help. While it is an investment, it doesn't have to cost thousands of dollars. Consider a site like Etsy – you can work with an artist to create something meaningful at a reasonable cost.

A professional logo offers the following ten benefits:
1. It creates a favorable first impression.
2. Boosts a farm's brand.
3. Visually tells your farm's story.
4. Increases credibility.
5. Clearly identifies your farm no matter where you are.
6. Communicates a farm is serious about its business.
7. Makes your farm seem established.
8. Communicates quality.
9. Indicates stability.
10. Communicates commitment.

When developing the artwork for your logo, answer the following questions:

- What is your farm's brand personality?

- What are your farm's core values or beliefs?

- What are the colors or symbols that represent those core values and beliefs, and why?

- What typeface represents those core values and beliefs?

- Is this logo unique?

There are four different types of logos. When creating a logo for a farm, think about the farm's brand story, personality, values, mission, purpose, and practices as you walk through the development process. Here are the four basic types of logos.

- **Wordmark Logo** is the simplest and least expensive logo. A wordmark is a typographic representation of a farm's name, such as the Disney logo, which is just their name written in the distinctive Disney font.
- **Lettermark Logo** builds on letters, typically initials from the farm's name, in the form of a graphic or image. An example of this is CNN, NASA, or the N for Netflix.
- **Brandmark Logo** creates a graphic representation of the business and relies on artistic imagery to invoke an emotional response or reaction. This is much like McDonald's use of the "Golden Arches."
- **Iconic Logo** is a blend of any of the other logotypes. This type of logo is effective in communicating your farm's brand. Think of the Pepsi logo, the Disney mouse ears, the four colored squares of Microsoft, etc.

Conclusion

Do not underestimate the power of symbols. A great logo provides a symbol of quality, farm practices, vision, and mission. Do not be afraid to spend money on a graphic artist who can create a quality logo for your farm. This money will be an investment in something that represents the totality of your farm.

Small Farm PR Strategy 5: Create an Award

"It doesn't matter how many times you win an award, it is always very special." ~ **Zinedine Zidane**

Giving awards positions a farm as a community leader. This builds credibility while building community. An award program is a tremendous tool for garnering local media attention. Most people, businesses, and organizations enjoy getting awards, and award events make excellent photo opportunities.

There are many types of awards, and your award ideas need not be limited to farm-related items. The awards you can give can be for fun, recognize community leaders, or promote a social cause. **Here are 10 award ideas any farm can implement.**

1. School Reading or Academic Awards. Encourage reading or academic achievement by contacting area schools. Offer prizes for student progress. There are many ways to structure this award, including grades, improvement, number of books read, number of words read, type of books, etc. This will involve working with a local school, and the partnering school can help determine the criteria.

This award requires prizes and those could include a farm tour, farm products, or other related items. This could be a monetary gift to the winner. The purpose is to create excitement for kids while encouraging families to visit your farm. This award can serve dual purposes. It can be a community service project, and it can build your farm's reputation.

2. School Science Fair. Farms are science in action. Sponsoring a science fair and offering an award is a great way to educate people on the science of farming. This allows students the opportunity to witness science in action while developing an understanding of how science directly affects their lives.

This science fair can include students from a single school, multiple schools, and even local colleges. This event can connect researchers, students, and practitioners. I personally know many farmers who complain that kids and people do not know where their food comes from. By hosting a science fair or supporting a school's science fair, you are making that connection and becoming part of the solution.

3. Homeschool Awards. Homeschoolers seldom receive public recognition. These students work just as hard as their counterparts. Your farm is a special place for these kids to visit and to learn. Many homeschool associations would make great partners for this event.

4. Loyal Customers. Invite your most loyal or favorite customers out for a night of fun and celebration. By providing your customers with food, drinks, and entrainment, you are building a strong bond between you and your customers.

5. Business Sustainability Awards. Look for businesses with sustainability programs and offer them an award. This provides local companies a reason to encourage employees to socialize off the clock and away from work in a fun setting.

6. Heirloom Produce Awards. Invite local gardeners to display their heirloom vegetables. This is a modern twist on a county fair competition. This event could be an opportunity to collaborate with groups such as your local chapter of The Master Gardeners.

7. Volunteer of the Year. This can help non-profit organizations recognize their volunteers. Your farm can provide a place for this ceremony, and by giving the location along with the plaque or certificates, you can ensure that your farm's name gets in front of people concerned about the local community.

8. Local Celebrity Award. This event is a great way to get the local newspaper, TV, or radio stations out with their cameras and microphones. In a way, you are feeding the egos of local celebrities, but you can make it more meaningful by tying this into a fundraiser for a local charity, sports team, or school group.

By making sure personalities from various sources of media receive an award, you are sure to get your farm's name mentioned positively.

9. Best Restaurant or Food Store Award. Promote restaurants or stores that buy your products. Find a reason to give an award for each restaurant that buys something from you. This strengthens the customer-supplier bond by giving a restaurant something to display on their wall or to post on their social media.

10. Best Blogger or Influencer Award. Local bloggers like to have their finger on the pulse of the local scene. This award will feed that emotion. Having some sort of best blogger award will also give these individuals something to blog about. Encouraging bloggers to write about your farm is terrific for your farm's reputation and brand.

Conclusion

There is an unlimited number of options for creating an awards program. Creating awards can be just a farm effort or an opportunity to collaborate with other organizations. Even if you do not create or give awards, when you host an award program at your farm, you are building bridges with your local community.

Offering awards allow a farm the opportunity to share its values with the community while building community. Organizations offering prizes and awards earn credibility while developing a community voice.

Small Farm PR Strategy 6: Sponsor a Competition

*"Build a lifestyle around your brand, and
the audience will follow." ~ Eva Chen*

The stoutest brands are lifestyle brands. Lifestyle brands appeal to people's values and idealized selves. Lifestyle brands work because they connect with people at multiple points and places in their life. A value or mission-driven farm is a perfect business to develop into a lifestyle brand.

Competition sponsorship is an excellent tool for building a farm brand into a lifestyle brand. These competitions can be fun or serious; either way, a farm is engaging with customers while positively building a community of farm supporters.

Competitions are a great press release item. By hosting a tournament, game, or another event, you can keep your farm's name in the news and in front of your customer. Also, competitions can introduce new customers to your farm, create new connections, and build ties with the local market.

Competition ideas for farms:

1. **Cardboard Box Races.** If you have a pond, lake, or river, this is an exciting family-friendly activity. There are many cardboard races across the country, and they tend to be popular events.

2. **Farm Olympics.** Farm Olympics is a modern twist on an old fashion field day. Farm Olympics activities include sack races, horseshoes, kickball, volleyball, etc. This is a wholesome, fun event for families, people dating, or anyone else looking for an active, clean source of entertainment.

   For a successful farm Olympic event, you need just 15 to 20 families to generate a crowd of 100 or more people. Other sources of customers could be area churches or religious groups who are looking for wholesome forms of entertainment.

3. **Fishing Derbies.** This exhilarating activity creates vivid and lasting, beautiful memories for kids and families. Fishing taps into people's need to connect with nature while building on nostalgia as parents remember time spent with their parents and grandparents.

   Many states have game and fish commissions that may be willing to assist with this event. Likewise, there are non-profit organizations and for-profit businesses that would be interested in working with you to host or sponsor this event.

A fishing derby is a great photo op for your farm. This event could have several families taking pictures of happy children with their catch while tagging your farm on social media. If you do not have the spot to host a fishing derby, consider asking your city if you could host a derby at a local lake or park. All you really need is to provide a few supplies and be the organizer of the event – people bring their own poles and bait.

4. **Animal Events.** This is an outstanding option for allowing people to connect with animals on a personal level. Many people, especially city or urban folks, seldom get the opportunity to interact closely with animals. This event allows people to get to know animals in a safe and fun manner.

   A farm in Dayton, Ohio, has a Farm Babies Festival. They charge $10 a car for families to see farm animals! A farm collective in Arkansas had a goat costume contest. A Christmas Tree Farm, also in my home state, has pig races during Pumpkin Patch and Christmas Tree season. These events are often part of a festival or larger event, but these can be standalone events to get people to visit a farm store.

   Have clear rules in place for people and animal safety. Plan your event with safety and respect for animals in mind.

5. **BBQ or Other Cooking Contest (chili, cheese dip, hot wings, fried chicken, etc.).** BBQ competitions have a cult following and are very popular throughout the country. If you raise protein, the entry fee for this event could be a purchase of your product to use during the competition.

   These events can quickly become an annual event. If you research cooking contests in your area, you will see these events attract large crowds. As a business, you want people attending these events on your farm, and as a farmer, you want the contestants to buy their food from you!

6. **Eating Contest.** There are many types of eating contests, as well as competitive eating associations. Competitive eating falls into a lifestyle brand, and a small farm is a great place to host this type of competition, especially if the event features a farm's products.

   A great strategy is to host this event with a product easily associated with a holiday or season. For example, a popular Fourth of July activity is eating watermelon. Raising melons and having a Fourth of July watermelon eating competition is a great marketing opportunity that provides fun for the whole family.

7. **Lumberjack Competition.** There are lumberjack associations that sponsor events across the nation, and a small farm could team up with one of these associations. This is a family fun activity easily connected to American myths and legends such as Paul Bunyan, John Henry, Pecos Bill, or any other frontier heroes.

   These high-energy events are great for farms with an adventurous brand personality. Lumberjack events include things like climbing trees, sawing logs, or chopping down trees.

8. **Gardening Competition**. Have a contest and give awards to the person who can hoe the fastest, pick the fastest, or plant the fastest. YouTube has a channel called Gardening Warz, which offers many great ideas for this concept.

   A gardening competition on the farm is more about creating an interactive event where people can see how food is grown. This would be an educational event disguised as a fun and light-hearted competition.

   There are serious garden competitions that Master Gardeners and other horticultural organizations sponsor. These events usually judge other people's gardens. You could always collaborate with one of these organizations and serve as a judge or have an awards ceremony on your farm.

9. **Dog Olympics.** People love their pets. Setting up an agility course and giving prizes for each event is a fun way to get people to spend the day with their furry best friend on the farm. If you raise produce, this competition can bring people to your farm during the non-growing season.

   Pet owners are a community; a Dog Olympics can be a meeting place for that community to grow. People may be worried about dogs and farm animals. However, with proper fencing, safeguards, and communication with attendees – animal and human safety should not be an issue.

10. **Chuckwagon Race.** This is a popular race event that involves horses and wagons. There are chuckwagon associations around the country that can help organize this event. This event can be huge. For example, a farm in Clinton, Arkansas, hosts the national chuckwagon race final and draws tens of thousands of people a year.

Conclusion

Hosting or sponsoring a competition is a great way to get a crowd on your farm. Competitions can range from super simple to crazy complicated. My advice is to pick something simple, small, and scalable. As competitions grow, so will your farm's visibility, image, and brand. The goal is to bring people to your farm for a fun activity! With just a few acres and some imagination and planning, there are unlimited opportunities.

Small Farm PR Strategy 7: Article Writing

"Writing is an exploration. You start from nothing and learn as you go." ~ E. L. Doctorow

Writing leads to deep thinking about values, mission, and purpose. Writing carries thoughts from one's imagination into the real world. Once in the real world, these ideas, concepts, and beliefs are sharable with anyone who can read. Writing is a process of reflecting and analyzing one's motivations and passions, which is why writing turns you into both a better farmer and a better human.

As your knowledge grows, share that knowledge with websites, blogs, magazines, newspapers, or other publications in search of content. By submitting regular articles or an occasional guest piece, you are creating opportunities to get your farm's name in front of a broader audience.

Best Practices for Small Farms: On Writing

Best Practice 1: Identifying Purpose. Articles fit into one of four purposes: to tell a story, to offer an opinion, to give information, and to persuade. Each use has a time and place, depending on your goal.

Storytelling, for many people, is the most straightforward form of writing. Storytelling typically uses a chronological order. If you are writing about your farm's history or purpose, storytelling may be the most effective way to share this information.

Stories are great for expressing a farm's values, mission, and vision while sharing the rationale for its processes. Storytelling will build your farm's connection to its community.

Opinion writing is useful for sharing views on social issues. There are many social, economic, and environmental issues facing farmers. Thoughtful opinions and good writing position you as a leader and thinker in your industry.

Opinion pieces are easy to write because you are free to express your emotions in the strongest terms possible. Opinion pieces tend to work backward from feeling to facts. Personal passions create the best opinions. The purpose is to promote a farm from a position of passion and purpose. This works because people are attracted to a passionate person's optimism and solutions.

Informative or expository pieces are practical writing. Common examples of this type of writing are news reports, instruction manuals, educational essays, how-to articles, and research papers. For your farm, this kind of writing is useful for recipes or farm guides. It is also helpful for explaining, for example, how to raise chickens or how you raise grass-fed beef.

A cookbook is a fun example of informative writing. People like new recipes. Writing recipes for farm products is a great way to promote a farm and its products. Taking this approach increases sales by providing examples and uses for farm products.

Persuasive articles can be marketing in disguise.
Commonly known as advertorials, this is one of the most challenging forms of writing because it sells something without using selling words.

This writing requires using an emotional appeal to guide people to logical decisions. When done correctly, this is one of the most effective methods of print messaging. Some publications charge for this, and some do not.

Best Practice 2: Analyze your Audience. The goal of writing articles is to get a farm's name in front of potential customers. When looking for places to submit articles, search for publications of interest to people who would be interested in your farm and write to that audience.

Best Practice 3: Topic Selection. Farmers can write articles on gardening tips, cooking, or environmental issues, among other ideas. Just make sure the topic is timely and relevant to the publication.

Best Practice 4: Sense of Humor. Humor is a bridge-building platform allowing a personal connection with readers. This tool enables people to make serious points without being offensive, and it opens the door for robust dialogue.

Greenville Kleiser says, "*Good humor is a business asset. It attracts and keeps friends. It lightens human burdens. It is the direct route to serenity and contentment.*" A little humor builds a lot of goodwill with potential customers while building a farm's brand.

Best Practice 5: Short and Simple. Most publications have maximum word requirements, with the most common being between 350 and 700 words. Most readers have a personal limit as to what they will read, and most people prefer brevity.

Best Practice 6: Practice. Good writing does not happen overnight. It takes practice. Growth as a writer comes from time, work, and diligence. As your farm grows, so will your writing and your personal growth. The key is you are always putting in the work of being a writer.

Anyone can write. It takes practice, and the more you write, the better writer you become. Writing is not an extraordinary skill that people are born with but something that develops and grows over time.

Conclusion

Writing articles is a great PR strategy. It positions a farm as an industry leader while giving voice to its social and environmental positions. Writing articles creates an opportunity for a clear definition of your purpose, passion, and practices, which makes you both a better farmer and human.

Small Farm PR Strategy 8: Charity Events

Owning a small farm means charity can literally begin at home. Hosting charity events is a great way to promote a small farm while doing something meaningful and worthwhile for the community.

People who attend charity events are concerned about social issues. These people are more likely to be interested in the farm to table movement and are more likely to spend more money with you than the general population.

A small farm is an excellent location for charity events. If the charity is a 501(c) (3) non-profit in good standing, a farm may treat this an "in-kind" donation. Supplying a location is beneficial for charities because it reduces their expenses while creating a fair market value tax deduction for a small farm.

Hosting charity events identifies a small farm as an established business. Many events are well suited for small farms, and here are 10 charity-related activities that do well in a farm setting:

1. Auction. Charity auctions come in many forms, including silent auctions or traditional live auctions complete with a fast-talking auctioneer. Many people like auctions, as these competitive events, tend to be fun, interactive, and socially engaging.

2. Polar Bear Plunge. This is a popular wintertime event allowing participants to pay money for the opportunity to jump into freezing water. The first organized and recorded polar bear plunge was in 1904 in Boston. Since then, polar bear plunges have increased in popularity.

A small farm with a water source such as a river, spring, pond, or lake is an excellent location for this event. A polar bear plunge is a great way to get people to visit a small farm during the winter months.

3. Art Shows. The arts are an indispensable element of culture. Many rural areas lack art museums or outlets for local artists. A small farm is a great place to host these events. Art is an outlet allowing people to express emotions, feelings, and hopes while reflecting on society.

People who attend art shows are community-minded and desire to contribute. This group of people is looking for community connections, and a small farm is an idyllic setting for an artist to share their creations with the world.

Children's art is another idea entirely – partner with the local school, especially in a rural area, to have a community-centered event with instant appeal. All parents love seeing their children's work.

4. Cultural Events. Cultural events provide an excellent opportunity for you to get your farm in front of people who are concerned about making the community a better place.

Cultural events are suitable for small, rural communities, and are great for humanity. The internet and social media have driven people into tribes instead of building community. Cultural events can be a bridge to bring together people who otherwise have little in common.

Examples could be a play, outdoor celebration for a holiday, a quartet of musicians, folk music or other music performances or types of specific art like sculpture or wreath making. This could also be interpreted literally by having events that celebrate a different culture-specific to your area, such as Native American culture, cultural aspects of the Ozark Mountain region, Amish culture, etc.

Cultural events, artists, and art organizations are an essential resource for community development. These events are great opportunities to engrain a farm into the local community's cultural fabric.

5. Fundraising Farm Dinners. Donating all or a portion of the money raised from a farm dinner to a local charity can highlight a farm's products while benefiting a local charity. Farm dinners allow people to deepen their connection with a farm while supporting a good cause.

These events can be simple or complex affairs. Preparation is vital. Even simple dinners will have many moving parts. For small farms new to food preparation, it is best to start small and simple and grow the complexity as the business grows.

6. Farm Run. 5k events or fun runs are always popular events. This type of event requires advanced planning and team effort. For many people, these events are part of a lifestyle, and hosting these events helps to define your farm as a lifestyle brand while getting people to your farm and doing something good for the community.

7. Farm Carnival. Farm carnivals are well-liked and fun spring and fall activities. The festive atmosphere of a festival is a great attraction that provides fun for people of all ages. Many churches, schools, and non-profit organizations use carnivals as fundraisers, and these are popular events for families or couples looking for a great date activity.

8. Night on the Farm. Similar to a night on the town, but with a farm twist, this could include candlelit picnics in the field with food and music, dancing, wine tasting, or any number of other activities.

9. Movies at the Farm. These movies could be in the field or in the barn. This is like movies in the park but in a more unique setting. This requires licensing. This ranges from $250 on up depending on the movie and event type. It is best to work with reputable licensing companies who can help with the event.

10. Scavenger Hunt. This is a great way to get people to explore a small farm. There are many different ways to approach a scavenger hunt. It could be a list of items they need to collect, chores they need to accomplish, a combination of the two, or something completely different such as geocaching.

Conclusion

Owning a small farm allows charity to begin at home. Small farms can play a pivotal role in supporting many social and environmental causes. Hosting or sponsoring charity events provides a community service while increasing a farm's visibility and image.

Small Farm Direct Marketing and Selling: 11 Proven Strategies

Direct marketing allows farmers to speak directly with customers. Marketing enables you to transform farm products from cheap commodities into valuable brands while turning consumers into customers. Direct marketing connects a farm with the world while ensuring profit from one's hard work. In direct marketing, you are advertising directly to your target consumer through promotional mail, email, or online advertising.

The primary goal of marketing is to sell more products to more people at higher prices. The second goal of marketing is putting the advice of Harvey Mackey into action who said, *"Dig your well before you're thirsty."* Marketing a farm means making connections with people and creating awareness for that farm. Effective marketing causes people to take one of four actions:

1. **Make a purchase.** Purchases drive profitability, allowing farmers to farm.
2. **Visit a website or follow social media pages**. Increased likes and more followers amplify your farm's visibility, which creates future customers.

3. **Call for more information.** This lets people know that your farm is approachable. This call for information is a glimpse into future marketing opportunities.
4. **Call for a quote**. This call can be the beginning of the sales process and provides future revenue.

Direct marketing builds on these four things:

- **Creating personal messages.** Direct marketing connects farms with a smaller, more manageable segment of the population than mass marketing, which allows for a more customized, straightforward and meaningful message.
- **Cost-effective.** Mass marketing is expensive. Direct marketing allows farmers to build a successful campaign on a limited budget.
- **Clear Communication**. Direct marketing offers greater control of the marketing message. This ensures accuracy and timeliness of a farm's communication.
- **Calculable**. Direct marketing makes tracking promotional effectiveness easier. This feedback allows timely changes to marketing efforts.

Direct marketing allows a farm's message to get in front of people interested in farm to table products and services. The Internet, especially social media, is a powerful tool and has its own chapter. This chapter focuses on traditional or "retro" direct marketing strategies, but with a modern twist.

Conclusion

Direct marketing is vital for small farm profitability. Many farmers complain about the obscene profits of the intermediaries and retailers. Direct marketing allows small farms to do something about this issue. Direct marketing delivers products directly to the end customer enabling farmers to earn more money.

In today's world, there is no need for small farmers to settle for scraps and leftovers. Small farmers have an opportunity to reshape how people purchase products if they reshape how they approach their business. Direct marketing increases profitability and secures the future of family farms.

Small Farm Marketing Strategy 1: Create a Newsletter

"Don't send out a newsletter just to send out a newsletter. One newsletter a year that is really interesting is more beneficial than 12 that are boring." ~ M. J. Rose

Newsletters target people interested in a specific topic, industry, or organization. A regularly published newsletter keeps people connected. A successful farm newsletter is relevant and packed with current information useful for a community of readers.

A small farm can use newsletters to accomplish two objectives. First, a newsletter is a tool used to maintain contact with current customers. This type of newsletter would include product information, seasonal offerings, recipes, and other farm happenings.

Secondly, a newsletter could focus on social or environmental issues that drive the farm's mission or practice. This could attract new farm customers. This newsletter would include articles on social or ecological concerns and a farm's stand on current trends and practices.

Either approach is excellent depending on overall marketing efforts. No matter the goal, here are eleven best practices for any newsletter.

Best Practices for Small Farms: Newsletters

Best Practice 1: Clear and Concise. A farm's newsletter should be short and down-to-earth. The best "marketing" newsletters should only take a few minutes to read. The average person is not interested in every little detail about your farm or your plans. Pick a few interesting items and share them distinctly and directly.

The most common newsletter mistake is length. In high school, teachers require students to write a minimum word count or length. Ignore that advice when creating a newsletter. Newsletters, as with other marketing materials, should have a maximum word count. Long unbroken text is overwhelming and daunting for readers. A general rule is to keep newsletters under 750 words.

Best Practice 2: Content. Good content keeps people's attention. When developing content, follow these six strategies.

- **Animal Stories.** People love animals, especially baby animals. Create a birth announcement section and treat this section just like the human birth announcement section of a local paper. Always include any new births or animal additions.

- **Farm Journey Stories.** What has your farm done lately? Share growth stories with customers, such as new buildings, processes, products, and services. Be human by sharing failures with the use of humor. Discuss what fell apart, why it fell apart, and lessons learned. Sharing good and bad stories makes a farm real.

- **Surveys**. Invite readers to take part in surveys. This is especially useful if your newsletter is electronic. These can be fun surveys, something used for market research, or both. Sharing survey results is a source of engaging content.

- **Blog Summaries**. If you are blogging, use this already created content in your newsletter. On the other hand, if you are creating a newsletter, you should blog. Many people will read content in one area and not another.

- **Tips, Tricks, and Tactics**. Include helpful advice on how to cook, store, or use farm products. Build on your customer interest in farm products. A newsletter allows space to explain product features and uses more completely.

- **Advice from Others**. Many people feel they have to contribute all the content; that is not true. For example, if you sell to a restaurant, the chef can write cooking articles. If you sell to a retail store, they can provide recipes.

Best Practice 3: Promote Business Customers. The newsletter should advertise businesses that buy from you. Advertising for customers strengthens those relationships. This promotion communicates a strong commitment to your customers while building their business.

These ads make your newsletter look professional. When people see ads, it implicitly gives the impression of professionalism. All forms of established media have ads in them. This is not a suggestion to go out and solicit advertisements but a suggestion to invest in your customers.

Best Practice 4: Audience Interests. For a farm newsletter consider the farm to table movement, sustainability trends, and the locally sourced crowd. People involved in these trends care about food production and the six broad categories outlined below.

- **Taste and nutrition.** People buy the food they enjoy eating. For food purchases, taste is the most important consideration, followed by nutrition. Healthy eating gets a lot of press, but tasty food sells the best. From a farm perspective, however, you have both.

    Each newsletter could highlight specific food and its taste attributes and nutrition. Providing recipes and food pairings is a great way to tie into this interest.

- **Environment**. According to the Leopold Center for Sustainable Agriculture, produce can travel 1,500 miles or more before it makes it to a local store! That is a lot of carbon released into the atmosphere. Locally grown food travels only a few miles, grown by people who are not pouring truckloads of chemicals onto the land and streams.

- **Community**. Farm to table people are part of a movement. A newsletter and your farm can be one of the tools that unite those people into a community. People have a desire for connection, and farmers need to build on that need.

  This connectedness is part of what transforms a commodity into a branded product. Big-Ag or mega-corporations do not care about the emotional wellbeing of their consumers. Building community is a competitive and sustainable advantage for small farms that the big players won't copy.

- **Seasonality**. People want to know what is in season. A farm newsletter should let people know what is in season and what is coming up next.

- **Local Economic Development.** Buying local keeps dollars nearby and makes the community better. When food travels 1,500 miles to get to a market, that means much of that purchase price is traveling 1,500 miles away from the local community.

- **Self-Reliance**. One of the goals of the farm to table movement is to create communities that can meet their own food needs. Ideally, this would eliminate the need for outside resources or long-distance transportation of food. Practically, that will not happen, but nonetheless, it is still a lofty goal worthy of pursuit.

Best Practice 5: Pick a Design or Template. Newsletter templates provide an appearing professional publication, which in turn builds credibility. The internet has many free or low-cost templates that are easily customizable, allowing you the opportunity to give your newsletter a better fit for your brand. Newsletter templates improve consistency while being easy to use. Don't forget photos in your newsletters. A picture with a brief description or paragraph goes a long way in personalizing your farm.

Best Practice 6: Proper Formatting. Templates help with formatting. Even with a template, use appropriate headers, subheaders, bullet points, and fonts. Proper formatting makes the newsletter not only easier to digest but more appealing and professional.

Headers and subheaders allow people to find topics of interest. Like headings, bullet points and lists make the text easier to scan. They also force you to make your message clear and concise, making it very easy for the reader to digest. Having said this, make sure your newsletter isn't overly formatted or so text-heavy that it needs a lot of headers, subheaders, or lists.

Newsletter fonts must be readable. Classic fonts such as Garamond, Times New Roman, Helvetica, or Arial are always good choices. Mixed fonts should be avoided as they make for difficult reading and look unprofessional.

Best Practice 7: Be Consistent. Effective newsletters need a regular publication schedule. Electronic newsletters are easy to schedule. A best practice is to create several editions in advance so they are ready to transmit at the push of a button. Regular publications show people you are dependable, and it provides customers something to look forward to reading.

Best Practice 8: Picture Perfect. Pictures are appealing storytelling devices. Stock images are great, but always include candid shots of your farm. Phones are a fantastic asset in this area.

With that said, an excellent standalone digital camera combined with picture editing software could be a wise investment. Great pictures have many uses beyond a newsletter. These pictures improve the visual quality of websites, social media platforms, and other marketing channels.

Best Practice 9: Call to Act. Encourage people to buy a product, visit your website for more information, and like or follow you on social media. Tom Hopkins, sales guru, says you should always be closing, and you should consistently be asking for your next sale. Follow his advice in your newsletter.

Best Practice 10: Grammar Matters. Proofread your newsletter. If you are not great with the written word, concentrate on using bullet points, write short sentences, and get a proofreader. There are professional proofreading services online, or you may be able to use a local English major who needs a little extra cash.

Best Practice 11: Contact Information. Let people know how to get in touch with you. Your newsletter needs to have your farm's phone number (with area code), website address, email, and social media platforms. This needs to be upfront and visible.

Conclusion

The best thing about your own newsletter is you control all the content. Your farm's newsletter is a great way to express your brand, values, and mission. The stories or reports in this newsletter allow people a glimpse into what makes your farm the special place it is.

Small Farm Marketing Strategy 2: Cold Calling

*"Selling is helping people to do what they're already inclined to do." ~ **Daniel H. Pink***

Cold calling is making contact with people who need to know about your farm but currently do not know about it. I am not advocating that you use this strategy to sell a few pounds of produce to individual customers; that approach would be time-consuming, and at best, will yield only a few small sales. I am advocating cold calling to larger customers such as restaurants, retail stores, schools, or roadside vendors who will purchase large amounts of products.

Cold calling is actually more personal than the name implies. Cold calling is the first step in building a relationship with a new person, and it usually starts with a phone call or visit to someone who fits your target market profile.

Effectual cold calling means being specific when targeting customers. The first step in cold calling is creating a list of businesses or organizations that are interested in small farm products. To do this, look for companies that advertise themselves as part of the farm to table movement.

When contacting restaurants, avoid peak times such as breakfast, lunch, and dinner. Traditionally, the slowest times for a restaurant is from 2:00 to 4:00 p.m. Google insights provides data as to when most businesses are busy, and this is excellent information to use when planning sales calls. Also, follow these four cold calling best practices:

Best Practices for Small Farms: Cold Calls

Best Practice 1: Research. Create a profile of whom you are going to call. This information needs to include the name of the business, hours, products, services, location, key personnel, and current suppliers.

This shows the person you are talking to that you care about, and this will make them more responsive to what you have to say. People will appreciate the effort made to understand their business, and this will create a better conversation.

Best Practice 2: Ask Questions. Be interested in your potential customer. Asking open-ended questions communicates interest; here are a useful dialogue creating questions:
- I noticed that you offer _____ products or _____ services. How are they working out?
- How long have you been in business?
- Why did you start this business?
- Tell me more about your day-to-day processes.
- Who are your current suppliers? What farms are you currently working with? How are they working out? What would you like them to do differently?

- Who are your customers, and what are they looking for?
- What role do you play in the decision-making process?

Morgan Ingram, a sales expert, puts it this way, *"The number one tip is to ask the right questions. Make sure your prospect's interests don't end along with the call. Use questions to keep the conversation and the relationship moving forward."* Cold calling must be customer-centered. When you ask questions and are genuinely concerned about your customer's needs, the rest of the sales process naturally falls in place.

Best Practice 3: Be Conservational. Scripts are clichéd, stereotypical, and impersonal. Instead of a fixed script, have an outline of essential questions and topics to cover. Using a script forces conversations, and forced conversations are seldom productive.

The best advice is to be sincerely interested in the other person and their business. People will know if you are just trying to get another sale or if you are trying to build relationships. In addition to being sincere, here are six "B's" to keep a conversation moving:
- **Be Positive.** People like people who are positive and see opportunities. Negativity is not an attractive attribute.
- **Be Complimentary**. Give the person a sincere compliment about their business.
- **Be Focused**. Selling is about matching needs with offerings. Focusing on customers is always a great business practice.

- **Be Respectful**. You are taking up part of this person's workday. Be mindful of that sacrifice. If the time is not right, offer to wait or to come back later when the time is suitable for the customer.
- **Be Polite**. Use your manners and show respect. Do not use vulgar or foul language, and do not say anything bad or negative about anyone.
- **Be Real**. Do not pretend to be something you are not to get the sale. It is better to forgo a onetime deal than it is to comprise who and what you are. Just move on to the next customer.

Best Practice 4: Get to the Point. The introduction needs to be quick, substantial, and straightforward. There is only one chance to make a first impression; therefore, make sure it counts.

In the first 15 seconds, you should introduce yourself, your farm, and your products. For example, "My name is Jason McClure, and I am with Ozark Family Farm. We sell Wagyu beef. I see that you are in the restaurant/retail business and that you are selling locally grown beef. How is that working out for you?"

These best practices, built on a sincere interest in your customer and a solid belief in your products, will earn you more customers creating more farm profitability. Small farmers work hard to produce quality products. For that reason, it is paramount to go out and sell that product.

Conclusion

Cold call selling is an excellent method to introduce a farm to new customers. Think of cold calling not as something to avoid but as something to embrace as a business building strategy.

Small Farm Marketing Strategy 3: Direct Mail

"Many a small thing has been made large by the right kind of advertising." ~ **Mark Twain**

Direct mail is one of the oldest forms of marketing, and it is still thriving. According to Forbes Magazine, response rates for direct mail averages 4.4%, with response rates reaching as high as 7% when using oversized envelopes. In contrast, the response rate for email is only .12% (less than one percent!).

According to a study conducted by UK Royal Mail, direct mail effectiveness comes from the physical connection people have with mail, and this connection can increase response rates by 30% when compared to similar digital advertising.

This is true for all demographics, including millennials. Gallup recently reported that 36% of people under the age of 30 look forward to checking their mailboxes every day, and 95% of 18-to-29-year-olds have a positive response to receiving personal cards and letters in the mail.

Even tech companies use direct mail. During the holiday season, I received mini-catalogs and other direct mail pieces from eBay, Amazon, and Wayfair. If large tech companies use direct mail, then it makes sense for small farms to use direct mail. Here are nine best practices for any direct mail program.

Best Practices for Small Farms: Direct Mail

Best Practice 1: Develop a List. This list needs to be limited to your target market. Individually stamps are inexpensive; however, when buying hundreds at a time, it is costly.

Current customers are a clear starting point for this list. If someone bought from you once, it makes sense to think he or she will buy again. Here are four ways to get customers' addresses:

- You could simply ask and tell them it is for future promotions, events, and specials.
- Have a contest or drawing where people must complete a form with their address.
- Create a loyalty program.
- From checks.

In addition to your current customers, look for directories that reflect your target market. For example, most towns or cities have a Chamber of Commerce with an online membership directory. These people tend to be professional and community-minded. If you belong to a trade, professional, or civic group that publishes directories, these are a great source of names of people who may be interested in your farm.

Best Practice 2: Invest in a List. Some companies create and develop lists based on consumer demographics and interests. Typically, companies rent lists for one-time use, but some companies sell the list. In many cases, these companies provide printing and mailing services, so it may actually make sense to rent the list instead of buying the list.

Best Practice 3: Consistency. Just like with any other form of advertising, people will need to see the message more than once. The first mailing might spark a little interest, but not enough interest to purchase. Consistently sending direct mail increases the likelihood that a purchase will be made.

Best Practice 4: Experiment. It is a wise practice to target different groups to see which audience is the most receptive to direct mail pieces. Many people think older people are more likely to purchase from direct mail; however, studies show that millennials are just as eager to receive this type of marketing.

To target your direct mailings, describe your typical customer using the following characteristics:

- Home location and type
- Interests
- Purchases
- Income level
- Gender
- Age

- Political leanings
- Religious beliefs
- Family status
- Social issues
- Education
- Other

Best Practice 5: Be Creative. As with any form of marketing, it pays to be creative. There are companies that custom manufacture different shapes, sizes, and colors of the mailing material. For example, if you sell vegetables, send your mailers out in a tomato, watermelon, or squash shaped envelope. If you sell beef or chicken, use animal-shaped mailers.

Pinterest, Instagram, or Facebook are excellent sources of inspiration for unique and attractive looking mailers. Look at what others have done and expand on their creativity.

An old twist that gets attention is handwritten envelopes. It's a time-consuming process, but it typically doubles and sometimes even triples response rates. When people get something handwritten, they assume it is from someone they know, and they are more likely to open it.

Best Practice 6: Create Good Copy. The direct mail text needs to be clean, easy to read with good flow. The design of your mailer determines the written copy. A letter is the most formal, and it must be grammatically correct. If it is a postcard or something less formal, bullet points and short statements will suffice.

All direct-mail must include a headline, offer, benefits, and a call to action. Headlines are to be simple, appealing, and succinct. Benefits must be clear, concrete, and convincing. The action must get the reader to do something tangible such as buying a product, liking or following your social media, or contacting you for more information.

The most important thing about copy is readability. Many people try to put all they can in a small space, thinking this is the most economical method. It is not. The most expensive ad copy is the ad copy that heads straight to the trash; the least costly ad copy is the copy that leads to a purchase.

Best Practice 7: Packaging Curiosity. Envelopes or packages that clearly contain a small gift encourage the opening. The little gift could be an ad specialty product such as a pen, magnet, or post-it notes.

Best Practice 8: Customer Focus. When developing direct mail, ask yourself the following four questions. What makes your customers happy? What does your customer want from you? What kind of farm products are they looking for? What can I do to fulfill those needs or wants?

Best Practice 9: Brand Building. All marketing efforts need to support, expand, and communicate your brand. Always include your logo and be consistent with font and color.

Conclusion

Direct mail advertising has stood the test of time because it is profitable. For a small farm, this is a great way to engage current customers or to attract new customers. Direct mail could be what makes your small farm a big business.

Small Farm Marketing Strategy 4: Neighborhood Marketing.

*"Nothing is better than going home to family and eating good food and relaxing." ~ **Irina Shayk***

People who live in subdivisions develop relationships with their neighbors. These people interact with the same people day in and day out.

Tapping into this community is a great way to build a community of customers. This is particularly true when targeting a subdivision designed for a particular population, whether it is for young couples, start-up families, or people who have shared interests such as golfing.

Many of these communities have a homeowner's association that organizes events like Christmas parties, garage sale weekends, or cookouts for the community. When a farm sponsors these activities, it is increasing the number of opportunities to interact with potential customers.

These connections increase your social media following and your customer base. If you operate a CSA (community supported agriculture) program, this is a great way to build subscribers. A neighborhood yielding 20 or 30 customers would be very profitable while streamlining operations by having a high concertation of customers in one area. You could offer delivery at a Community Park or at home.

For small farms, direct marketing beef, chicken, or pork is a great way to develop a "sales route" to move more product. Your farm could make door-to-door sales or set up at a designated place in the neighborhood on a specific day. Another option is to encourage neighbors to split animals, as most city folks do not have freezer space for a large animal.

For small farms that operate pumpkin patches, Christmas tree farms, or other agritourism related specialties, this is an idea that gives the community something to experience together. To encourage this, consider offering a group discount on a specific day.

Neighborhood farmers markets are popping up across the country. I have attended a few of these with great success. If there is not a neighborhood farmers market in a viable neighborhood, approach the homeowner's association about developing a market.

Conclusion

When you market to a subdivision, you are doing more than marketing to a community, you are creating a community.

Small Farm Marketing Strategy 5: Farm Catalog

"Catalogs bring a world of possibilities to a mailbox."
~ Granddad McClure

Catalogs have been part of American culture for nearly 200 years and have broad appeal to many different demographics. In the beginning, catalogs targeted middle-class women, but over time catalogs have grown to target just about any demographic selling any product imaginable.

Catalogs are nostalgic. I remember the Sears wish book, a colossal color catalog that arrived in our mailbox in Pine Snag, AR. This modern marvel brought a world of possibilities to us backwoods, country folks.

This catalog connected generations. The old-timers told stories of how everything they needed for their original homesteads was purchased from the Sears catalog brought by train to Searcy, AR, and then by wagon Pine Snag.

The 1980s and beyond brought technological changes to retailing, logistics, and the moving mass of merchandise that slowly chipped away at the market share of the Sears catalog, and now the Sears catalog has been lost to history and has been replaced by the mammoth known as Amazon.

Some people say it is sad that Amazon killed the Sears catalog. I content it is unfortunate that Sears did not adjust to new economic realities and did not adopt new technologies and ways of doing business.

I mention the decline of the Sears catalog to point out that even the biggest, seemingly most durable, and most iconic businesses can fail. It is not just small farms or companies that face demise in the change of new market forces, but all companies can fail.

In 1995, Amazon was housed in a garage, and it just sold books; therefore, if you own or have access to property, barn, and farm products, you have much more to offer than the Amazon of 1995 had to offer.

Catalogs still have a place in marketing. Amazon sends out catalogs. Granted, these are not a thousand-page Sears style catalog with every product imaginable, but it is usually a small Christmas catalog advertising a few essential products.

Most people read catalogs. Personally speaking, I will read a catalog even if it takes a few weeks and a few reminders from my wife to read it. I do not always order something, but I usually look at it. When I do order, I never use the order form in the catalog, but I visit the company's web site to place an order.

Depending on the farm brand's personality, a catalog can be a great brand enhancer. A small farm should not recreate the all-encompassing Sears and Roebuck catalog; a small farm should create a small catalog focused on its most profitable products.

Catalog marketing is best for shelf-stable products such as frozen meats or value-added products such as jams, jellies, salsa, cheeses, etc. A catalog creates the impression that a farm is established, professional, and competent.

Catalogs may not be as expensive as you think. As of this writing, Uprinting.com offers 250 catalogs for $1.35 each or a total of $332.50. Depending on what you sell, this could be a good investment. Here are eight best practices for catalog marketing.

Best Practices for Small Farms: Catalog Marketing

Best Practice 1: Brand Visualization. A catalog is a great visual representation of a farm's brand to customers. This includes selecting artwork, graphics, text, layout, and other symbolism to support the brand. Think of a catalog as a picture book that visually expresses a farm's mission, values, and practices.

Best Practice 2: Catalog Design. Catalogs can be slick and modern or old-timey and classic – or anywhere in between. The cover is the first impression of the catalog, and it needs to convince people to open and read it. The cover must be aesthetically appealing while communicating what is inside. Catalog interiors should have a user-friendly layout and design with appropriate white space.

Best Practice 3: Catalog Content. Catalog content must be clear, concise, and easy to read. The best catalog content is educational or entertaining. The content must provide customers all the necessary information required to make a purchase. Ordering information including website and phone number with transparent pricing should be in easy to read tables.

Best Practice 4: Images and Graphics. If a catalog is not visual, it is not going to be effective. Most people use stand-alone pictures of their products. Product pictures are okay, and they do have their place; however, the best photos are candid pictures featuring people enjoying farm products in real-life settings.

If your farm brand is old fashioned, consider using drawings or pictures converted to drawings for images. There is nothing wrong with a retro-looking catalog. A catalog that looks like it is from the 1800s will feel different from most modern catalogs and draw more attention than a slick, new modern looking catalog.

Best Practice 5: Create Urgency. Offer customers a discount if they order within a few days. Include expiration dates for items and offers to make people think that offers are only for a limited time. People tend to be more motivated if they believe they are going to lose something than if they are going to gain something.

Best Practice 6: Make it Easy. Ordering must be simple. A farm must have a website, and people should be able to purchase from the site. If you are going to take orders by mail, make sure your mailing address is easy to find. If you are going to accept orders by phone, make sure your number is easy to find. Also, include hours you are open and hours that you take phone calls.

Best Practice 7: Supporting Role. A print catalog should not be your only marketing tool. A catalog should support a farm's other marketing efforts. Successful businesses, including farms, treat marketing as a multi-channel practice; therefore, farm catalogs need to drive customers to a farm's website or social media platforms.

Best Practice 8: Analyze and Adjust. Analyzing catalog performance, as well as the rest of your marketing activities, must be a part of an ongoing improvement plan. This data will help you cut products from your product mix or give you ideas of new products or services for the farm to offer.

Conclusion

Many companies, including tech companies such as Amazon, use catalogs because catalogs work. Catalogs provide customers with ideas for new products for themselves or gifts for friends and family. Small or mini-catalogs can extend a farm's brand, create new customers, and increase revenue.

Small Farm Marketing Strategy 6: Newspaper and Classifieds

"Advertisements contain the only truths to be relied on in a newspaper." ~ **Thomas Jefferson**

Classified ads are useful for marketing small farm products. Classified ads have been selling products in America since 1704 when the Boston News-Letter posted a classified advertisement for an Oyster buyer. Since then, classifieds have sold virtually everything - including farm products.

Many newspapers offer free or low-cost classifieds. In my first year selling produce, I placed classified ads in all the local newspapers and classified papers within an hour's drive from my farm. All but one of these ads was successful, and most of these ads connected me with resellers, retail, and wholesale customers who made larger purchases.

A few of these publications ran display ads that only cost $15.00 a week for a six-week commitment. These ads did well, so I kept running them until the end of the growing season. Part of the reason they worked was consistency. The other reason they work is people looking to buy local produce tend to use print media to find local farmers.

Online advertising is trending; however, it is easy to spend $15.00 a week or more for keywords. Local print allowed me to reach up to 30,000 people a week, depending on the publication for a fixed cost.

Granted, nationally and state-wide published newspapers are declining in readership. According to Journalism.org, *"The estimated total U.S. daily newspaper circulation (print and digital combined) in 2017 was 31 million for weekday and 34 million for Sunday, down 11% and 10%, respectively, from the previous year."*

With readership on the decline, why would a person want to spend money advertising in a newspaper or a classified paper? The answer is the cost, reader loyalty, and local reach. This will change each year and will need to be evaluated, but for the current time, there is still value in this kind of advertising.

Declining readership means the remaining readers are immensely loyal. This means the person reading the local newspaper is really engaged with the paper versus someone subscribing to something and not reading it.

Many people read their local newspaper to keep up with local news. The New York Times, USA Today, The Wall Street Journal, etc. are not posting lists of local honor roll students or a feel-good story about a local FFA kid who won an award. It is the small, local paper publishing those stories.

Local newspapers provide a valuable service to the local community. Advertising locally supports local news. You are also keeping advertising dollars local while promoting your farm to nearby people.

Best Practices for Small Farms: Classified Ads

Best Practice 1: Selection. Pick the right publication. Typically, the larger the classified section, the better the results. I used a local newspaper that had a weak classified section that cost much more than other publications. I did not get a single response even though I paid double for the ad.

I use the same ad in a classified trader publication, and I got a tremendous response. In other words, I spent half of what I did for the traditional newspaper but got at least three times the results.

Best Practice 2: Readership. Ask yourself who reads this publication and why it is read? How many people read it? The paper's media kit or website has this information. Do not advertise in any publication without this information.

Best Practice 3: Category Selection. The fact that classifieds have categories is a plus, according to Jay Levinson, author of Guerrilla Advertising. *"Classifieds are powerful because they allow you to pinpoint customers."* Monitor the categories used by other local farms. How does their category work for your farm? If you do not see a category you like, ask the paper to create a category. I have done this, and as long as the request is bonafide, they will typically create a new category.

Best Practice 4: Price. Think in terms of return on investment. A starting point is to calculate cost per reader. To get this number, take price and divide it by the number of readers. The lower the cost per reader, the better the investment.

The ultimate determiner is actual sales. If a cheaper option does not yield any additional sales, then it is an expense. If a more expensive option generates additional revenue over the cost, it is an investment. This is a business transaction; do whatever option puts the most dollars in your pocket while taking the least amount of money out of your pocket.

Best Practice 5: Message. The headline needs to be bold in both message and text. Spend as much time as required with this task. Analyze other ads and build your headline from these examples. With classifieds, shorter is better, and you should keep working to make your headline as short as possible while conveying your message.

Best Practice 6: Concise. Classified ads must be as short as possible while communicating all the fundamental information. Use abbreviations, short words, and avoid flowery language. Think like a telegraph operator and use only sentence fragments – just make sure they are readable!

Best Practice 7: Online. Virtually all print media have websites. Make sure your print ad goes online. Online ads can be longer and can include hyperlinks to your website or social media accounts.

Also, use websites such as Craig's List, Facebook Marketplace, or other free options. Since they are free, one new customer makes them worth the effort.

Best Practice 8: Call to Action. A classified ad needs to prompt the reader to call for more information, place an order, visit a website, or visit the farm.

Best Practice 9: Contact. A classified ad needs to have your contact information, including your phone number with area code and your web address. Do not make it a challenge for people to contact you.

Conclusion

Classified ads are useful for local advertising. They are not as flashy as internet advertising, but they can be very economical. The key is selecting the right classifieds for what you are selling.

Small Farm Marketing Strategy 7: Magazine Ads

"Marketing is designed to bring people into something."
~ Sue Naegle

Magazines exist for virtually every hobby, interest, or lifestyle. This makes niche magazines an excellent choice for small farm advertising. Currently, locally grown and farm to table magazines are gaining in popularity in many markets, so it is safe to say that the readers of these magazines are interested in locally grown food and small farms.

Magazines create clear and colorful images for readers. The glossy pages with full-color pictures make magazines a terrific brand-building tool. In addition to the graphic imagery, magazines are limited in scope and topics, and most magazines have a distinct target audience.

It is safe to say that the readers of Guns and Ammo are interested in guns and ammo. It is safe to say the readers of Guitar World are interested in guitars. It is safe to say the reader of car magazines are interested in cars. It is safe to say that magazine readers have an above-average interest in a given topic.

Five Benefits of Magazine Advertising:

- Readers physically touch magazines, solidifying the connection between the magazine and the reader. This physical connection creates a stronger emotional bond.

- Magazines are subscription-based connections with individuals who share a common interest and whose interest is deep enough to spend money on that topic.

- Most print magazines have an online version expanding the reach of your advertising dollars.

- Magazines have a long shelf life. Many people collect magazines, and even more, people will reread or save articles from their favorite magazines.

- Multiple magazines exist whose readers are interested in your farm.

Best Practices for Small Farms: Magazine Advertising

Best Practice 1: Correct Choice. Select the right magazine. The narrow focus of magazines usually means advertising is either a hit or a miss. Think carefully about the readers of the magazine. I once advertised in a magazine that went to agricultural people and did not get a single response. I used the same ad in a local food magazine and got several inquiries.

For a farm, I would recommend looking for farm to table magazines, locally grown magazines, or local food magazines. Other magazines may work, but these will be your best bet.

Best Practice 2: Circulation .vs Cost. Magazine ads can be expensive. It costs money for the color pictures, glossy pages, and sales commissions. Before you purchase an ad, determine the cost per thousand to see if it makes sense.

Best Practice 3: Contribute. Local magazines are always on the lookout for content. A magazine feature or story about your farm, even if it is paid, is a great use of your advertising dollars. This article is a tool that can garner future press and is a great news item for your website. Local magazines are always on the lookout for content, and if you can write articles or columns for a local magazine, you might earn some free press.

Best Practice 4: Reader Attention. Catch the reader's attention. The headline needs to attract the reader, and the headline is where you should invest most of your creative energy. As always, include your logo and graphics or other images that reinforce your brand's story.

Best Practice 5: Concise. Magazine ads should not be another article unless it is an advertorial. Start a binder of magazine ads that grab your attention and study these ads. Learn from advertisers who make their ads clear, concise, and catchy.

Best Practice 6: Content Purchase. Advertorial marketing is an ad disguised as content. In 2007, Reader's Digest researched the usefulness of advertorials. Their research found advertorials were 81% more effective than traditional magazine ads. This research also revealed readers are 500 times more likely to read an advertorial than a standard article.

For advertorials to be effective, they must align with the magazine's objective. Secondly, they must be of use to the reader. A great advertorial explains (or tells) more than it sells.

Finally, the article must read like a magazine article. You may provide the content or outline, but many times the magazine editors will have the final say and will do much of the writing.

Best Practice 7: Contact information. This keeps showing up because it is essential. When people read your magazine ad, your contact info must easy to read and locate. Include your phone number, website, and social media handles.

Conclusion

Magazines, especially local magazines, are a great way to communicate your brand story to people who are interested in farm products. Select magazines carefully so that your time and money are not wasted.

Small Farm Marketing Strategy 8: Value-Added Products

"In a marketplace where it's so easy to produce products, where your competitors can essentially match you on the product itself, you need to have something else. You need to have an added value, and that added value is the identity, the idea behind your brand." ~ **Naomi Klein**

Value-added products increase farm profitability. Developing value-added products is an opportunity to test just how big an idea can grow. Big ideas are going to come with big obstacles. The government heavily regulates agriculture and food processing, creating many unnecessary barriers to entry disguised as consumer protection. In reality, the goal is to protect big business.

The good news is some value-added products can be homemade, but many other value-added products are going to require equipment, permits, infrastructure, new skills, and new ways of thinking. These obstacles will take time, money, and dedication to overcome.

Do not be scared of value-added products. Be excited about the opportunity. Many farmers, both large and small, complain about the money made by processors, retail, or restaurants; however, only a few farmers take action to earn that money.

Developing value-added profits pulls you up from the rank of complaining farmer and promotes you to the position of industry leader. You have the same potential to be as successful as anyone else, and all it takes to be successful is just one good idea executed well.

This section includes a list of value-added products. This is not an exhaustive list, but something to help you brainstorm. Currently, there are farmers making money from the ideas on this list. Some of the ideas may simply make your farm unique and give people a reason to not forget you. So, some ideas, even if not done on a large scale, are still worthwhile in setting you apart. As you read this list, remember to check local permits, laws, and codes before bringing one of these ideas to market.

- **Baby Food.** This will require a commercial kitchen but could be a great business. People care about what they feed their babies, and are willing to spend money on healthy baby food from a source they trust.

- **Baked Goods.** Most states allow people to bake breads, cakes, cupcakes, and certain types of pies without a commercial license or equipment. A common requirement is the sale of these items to be limited to farmers markets or roadside stands. However, there are several examples of people who have built this into a bonafide standalone business.

- **Candy.** Typically, this is limited to baked hard candies. The laws on this vary by state. This is an excellent add on item for farmers markets or roadside stands.

- **Canned Food.** Most states require a commercial kitchen, but this is usually an untapped market. Once the commercial kitchen requirements are met, waste turns into profit and generates year-round revenue.

- **Cheese.** Think artesian cheeses from a local dairy. The declining dairy industry has very little chance of rebounding. However, profitable small dairies exist by turning milk into specialty cheeses or other value-added products.

- **Chocolate Covered Dried Fruits and Nuts.** This is typically a good seller at most farmers markets, roadside stands, and farm stores. This is a great way to sell fruit at a higher price while allowing customers to enjoy something delicious while they shop.

- **Cut flowers.** Cut flowers, especially sunflowers, are always great sellers, and they make things more attractive. Flowers are great for creating repeat business and attracting attention.

- **Dog Treats.** People love their pets. Some states allow this under their cottage law, while other states require a commercial kitchen. There are many people whose pets are their children and who are willing to spend big money on their pets.

- **Donuts.** This easy to eat treat is something everyone likes. I have an Amish neighbor who makes a nice income just selling a glazed cake donut at the town square.

- **Dried Fruit.** Depending on your state's laws and regulations, this may require a commercial kitchen. Dried fruit makes a great snack, and many people view it as a healthy alternative to candy or processed sweets.

- **Dried Grain Mixes.** These are mixes that may be used whole, soaked, cracked, or ground into flour for baking. Most people selling dried grain mixes purchase bulk grains and make the mix themselves. Some states require a commercial kitchen for mixing, and some do not.

- **Dried Soup Mixes.** Most often, this is vegetarian soup mixes with dried beans. This usually requires a commercial kitchen, even though there is no cooking involved. Many people buy bulk dry ingredients and then make custom mixes using their own recipes packaged under their farm's name.

- **Farm Swag.** Selling farm logo items turns your farm into a lifestyle brand. This includes T-shirts, hats, mugs, etc.

- **Fruit Butter.** Fruit butters get their name because it spreads like butter. Fruit butters are cooked whole or halved unpeeled fruits. This is a superb item for branding with your farm's logo. Fruit butters do not contain a gelling agent, and their thickness comes from reduction while cooking. Many cottage laws allow for the production of fruit butter.

- **Fruit Preserves, Jams, and Jellies.** These products allow for year-round sales. These make exceptional gift items and tend to do great in farm stores or when sold online. Most cottage laws allow for this when sugar is used, but require a license when a sugar substitute, such as Splenda, is used.

- **Garlic.** This is the only universal spice. Every type of cuisine uses garlic in some of its dishes; however, most grocery stores only carry a few kinds of garlic. Dried garlic has a long shelf life, and given the many types of heirloom garlics, you can easily have a unique product promoted under your farm's brand.

- **Herb Blends.** Mixing and matching fresh or dried herbs is a great way to increase the value of your herb plants. Herb blends are popular with people concerned with their salt intake. Typically, fresh herbs do not require a license, but dried herbs may require a commercial kitchen.

- **Honey.** There is a huge demand for locally sourced honey. I know from experience that honey is a great seller and a high-profit item. When I have honey, I sell out.

- **Horseradish.** Horseradish is an easy to grow root that can survive just about any growing condition. Horseradish sauce is a popular condiment that has very few local options. This would be an outstanding complement for farmers who sell beef or pork products.

- **Ice cream.** People love treats. This capital-intensive process can be profitable. A popular niche in this category is goat milk ice cream for people who are lactose intolerant. This requires a commercial kitchen.

- **Ketchup.** This condiment has been making appearances as a locally grown and sourced item. This usually requires a commercial kitchen.

- **Maple Syrup.** This is a very high dollar product. If you live in an area with maple trees that you can tap, you can tap into a vast market. Maple syrup sells itself.

- **Pickles.** A popular food item that people use as a condiment or snack. For value-added products, think beyond cucumbers - consider okra, peppers, or other vegetables. Many states require a commercial kitchen for pickle production.

- **Popcorn.** This is one of the most popular snacks in America, but there are very few locally sourced providers of popcorn.

- **Potato and Vegetable Chips.** These snacks provide a great opportunity to break into the snack food business. Many retailers are looking for locally sourced food items, and these chips could be a lucrative market for the right producer.

- **Potpourri.** This is a great gift item. Potpourri comes from dried flowers, pinecones and bark mulch with fragrant essential oils added. Once packaged, potpourri offers a variety of sales channels, including the farmers market, craft shows, or wholesale to retailers.

- **Precooked or Premade Meals and Salads.** This requires a commercial kitchen. However, restaurants and grocery stores sell these items. Why not cut out the intermediary and keep the profit for yourself.

- **Retail Meat Cuts.** This usually requires state licensing, as well as processing at a USDA, inspected facility. There will be some logistical work and other requirements, but meeting these requirements will allow you to capture more value for your work.

- **Salsa.** Most states will require a commercial kitchen. Some businesses will use your recipe and put your label on the jar. This allows you to spend your time marketing salsa instead of making salsa.

- **Tomato Sauces.** This is like canning and will have the same commercial kitchen requirements. However, the demand for locally sourced food items can make this a big thing.

- **Yogurt.** People who eat yogurt tend to be more health aware and concerned with sustainability issues. This makes yogurt an excellent choice for a value-added product. As with cheese and ice cream, there are small diaries that have turned a profit by focusing on this niche.

Conclusion

Value-added products are a great way to expand your farm's business. Some of the ideas listed require a commercial kitchen, which can be expensive. However, there are options such as renting a commercial kitchen from a restaurant, catering company, or even a church. Also, some states have innovation hubs, or some USDA offices have commercial kitchens for producers to create and experiment with value-added products.

Small Farm Marketing Strategy 9: Develop a CSA

"To make agriculture sustainable, the grower has got to be able to make a profit." ~ Sam Farr

Community-supported agriculture (CSA) is a pre-season agreement for a portion of a farm's future harvest. The goal of this agreement is to share the farming risk while providing a CSA member a supply of farm-fresh food. Some farms offer a whole, half, or quarter subscriptions. Other farms offer family, couple, or individual shares.

Many farms require people to make the first subscription payment in advance. This helps to cover farming expenses while ensuring the person is serious about participating in the CSA. I would encourage getting the first payment in advance; many well-intended people will not follow through otherwise.

This agreement shares the risk; therefore, subscribers need to be aware that things may not go as planned. Also, farmers need to respect that these people are sharing in the risk by making sure subscribers share in the bounty. With my CSA, I make sure my subscribers get the best quality produce and the biggest possible bang for their investment.

Recruiting Subscribers. It takes advertising to get subscribers. CSA advertising begins in the winter and should continue until planting or all the subscriptions have sold. Here are seven ways to recruit members:

- **Current Customers**. These people know you, your farm, and your practices. Tell them that you value the relationship, and your goal is to get them the best product for the best price next growing year, and that a CSA is the best tool for that goal.

- **Social Media Groups**. Advertise on local community or yard sale pages. This is usually a low cost or free method of advertising.

- **Your Network**. Ask friends, family members, co-workers, previous co-workers, or anyone else. Let people know you are starting a CSA, and you are looking for subscribers.

- **Chamber of Commerce**. Virtually all chamber of commerce organizations posts their membership directory. Contact your local chamber and offer to work them to create a CSA for their members.

- **Civic Groups or Churches**. Contact these groups and offer deliveries when they meet or at another suitable time.

- **Workplace CSA**. Contact the benefits managers or human resources department of large employers in the area. Offer this as a free benefit to their customers.

- **Marketing**. This book is full of marketing tips and strategies for your farm. Apply those concepts when developing and marketing your CSA.

Best Practices for Small Farms: The CSA

Best Practice 1: Quality. CSA subscribers are investing in you. These people deserve your best efforts and products. Quality needs to extend beyond your products and into your packaging. Use high-quality boxes, bags, and packing materials.

Best Practice 2: Clearly Defined Expectations. A CSA is a relationship, and productive relationships have clearly defined expectations. Here are seven items that need setting when developing a CSA:

- Contact information
- Payment and refund policy
- Delivery dates and location(s)
- Liability waivers
- Quality and quantity expectations
- Share definitions
- Production methods and plans

Best Practice 3: Be Consistent. Consistently providing excellent service and quality products is essential. The products are going to change with the season, but the delivery dates, times, location, and service must be consistent.

Best Practice 4: Establish a Core Group. The 80/20 rule states that 80 percent of your business will come from 20 percent of your customers. People will drop out of your CSA for a variety of reasons, but if you develop a loyal group, you have the foundation for a very profitable business.

Best Practice 6: Don't Over Book. For me, this is the most laborious practice to implement. However, it is necessary to say no to people so that you may maintain quality, service, and consistency. There are only so many hours in a day, and a garden can only produce so much. The best business practice is to work within these constraints while keeping track of these people for next season. Being a sold-out CSA is better than not delivering on quality and quantity for your existing members.

Best Practice 5: Community. When people purchase a CSA share, they are not buying produce, meat, cheese, or other farm product. They are buying a relationship with a farmer. Creating a community builds loyalty while forming lifelong friendships.

Best Practice 6: Individualize. Most CSA programs have a one-size fit all approach. The problem with this approach is it makes the farm and its operation the center of the relationship. The customer should be at the center of the relationship. Operational efficacy is essential, but the best systems are useless without a customer to buy products.

Whenever possible, make minor changes for individuals. Individualizing the experience can be as simple as putting a person's name on their box or swapping out veggies based on customer preferences.

If you have a CSA with 20 people or more, there will be customer preferences that will balance out throughout the season. Make these changes. It only takes a few minutes, but those few minutes can earn you a customer for life. If customer A likes beets but not carrots, and customer B likes carrots but not beets, adjust it, and let them know you made this change.

Best Practice 7: Give a Little Extra. Operate your CSA out of an abundance mentality versus a scarcity mindset. When you operate out of abundance, it builds goodwill with people, and they will reward you with future business. People like extra goodies, and I find giving these goodies away is an excellent use of products that are not otherwise moving.

Best Practice 8: Ask for Referrals and Reviews. The best CSAs will lose people each year. During the year, ask people for referrals for the following year, and reward them for these referrals. It could be monetary, free product or free flowers with their next order. Also, as people praise your CSA ask if they would mind sharing that praise online.

Best Practice 9: Seek Feedback. Businesses that do not evolve or adjust to changing economic forces are doomed to failure. One of your major challenges as a business owner is to predict future trends while improving your current farm operations. Talk and listen to your customers and ask questions about:

- Favorite products
- Least favorite products
- Location/delivery
- Packaging
- Value
- Service expectations
- Other improvements

Best Practice 10: Price Right. Price your CSA like you would any other branded product that is superior in quality. When pricing a CSA subscription, think about the emotional impact of the price. Extreme pricing is always problematic. If the price is too high, people cannot afford it; if the price is to low, they will not value it.

The subscription needs to be manageable in terms of your customer's food budget. I start by thinking about how much a person would spend each week at a farmers market to gauge my starting point.

For example, would it be reasonable for an individual to spend $10 to $20 a week at a local farmers market? Would it be feasible for a couple to pay $20 - $30 a week? Would a family spend $50.00 a week? I then determine what the market will support, and then I publish my price. I also remember it is always easier to lower prices than to raise prices; therefore, I start on the high end and give discounts as needed.

Best Practice 11: Product Mix. People have a relationship with their food. In relationships, people strive for a balance between predictability and novelty. Certain conventional items such as tomatoes, lettuce, squash must be included to meet the customer's need for predictability and familiarity.

The novelty proportion is a significant part of the attraction of buying local. It is the customer's opportunity to get something different. A great practice is to include a few heirlooms along with a few rare or unique vegetables to give people something new to try and talk about. You can even include information on rare items or how to incorporate them into a meal. For more information about heirlooms, check out my book *Heirloom Style Produce for Fun and Profit* on Amazon.

Conclusion

CSAs are popular for farmers and customers. A CSA requires planning and preparation but can be mutually beneficial for farmers and customers. The key to success is to market your CSA, clearly define the expectations, maintain consistency, and provide excellent customer service.

Small Farm Marketing Strategy 10: Farmers Market

"What makes the farmers market such a special place is that you're actually creating a community around food."
~ Bryant Terry

Farmers markets provide a place for farmers and customers to connect and to build relationships. This is the first place people think of to sell their products when they begin a farm or homestead. It is a unique place to connect with like-minded growers and buyers, and it really does create a community around food.

Farmers markets have their place, but I do not think farmers should solely rely on them. Let me explain my hesitation. When selling at a farmers market, you must play by their rules, and these rules do not always make sense. Besides, you are entering a crowded market place with lots of competition. It is a high-risk action for a moderate benefit at best. Attendance at any farmers market is dependent on the weather, and a stormy day can waste a week's worth of produce.

With that said, some small farmers love farmers markets and have successfully built a business around these events. I also know despite my concerns and criticisms I will continue to have a presence at local markets.

The best farmers markets are popular and dynamic local or regional destinations with a loyal following. At these markets, farmers can do quite well financially. A word of caution, these markets are often challenging to break into, and often have long waiting lists.

Sadly, some farmers markets are nothing more than a few people sitting in a parking lot trying to peddle a few turnips. At these markets, farmers struggle to sell much of anything and do poorly financially. This is why it is crucial to pick the right farmers market.

As plans are being made, visit as many farmers markets as possible. Use the internet to guide this endeavor. Pick farmers markets that have the best reviews, the most likes, and the best internet presence. Research in advance! Once again, the best markets have waiting lists, mileage, or growing requirements for vendors. Keep in mind the best market for you may not be the closest to you.

Leigh Adcock, executive director of the Women, Food, and Agriculture Networks, says, *"Every market has its own culture and vibe."* **The market culture is very important**. A market's culture will not change just because a new vendor is showing up. As you visit markets, talk to vendors and customers with the intent to determine whether you will compliment that market's culture and vibe.

In some markets, vendors are collaborative and support others; in other markets, vendors are highly competitive and work to sabotage new vendors. I have built friendships at some markets and learned valuable growing advice; at another market, a grower came to me on my first day there and explained, quite rudely, why he did not think I should not be there. I returned the next week and every week until the end of the season.

Best Practices for Small Farms: Farmers Market

Best Practice 1: Differentiate. What are you going to do better than your competition? What will give you an edge in that market? Think in terms of promotion, package design, and customer service.

Best Practice 2: Tell Your Story. The story that needs telling is your farm's mission, purpose, and history. People buy into stories, and stories allow people to make an emotional connection. Your story makes you unique. Competitors can replicate your products and services; however, they cannot copy your story.

Best Practice 3: Be Efficient and Effective. Develop a system for organizing, transporting, and displaying your products. It is an excellent idea to develop and use a setup and teardown checklist. This list needs to include things such as change, canopy weights, bags, containers, banners, marketing materials, etc. The checklist should be used while packing for the market and setting up at market.

Best Practice 4: Timely Transactions. Serving more customers means bringing home more money. The goal is to speed up transaction time without sacrificing customer service. To speed up transaction time, use a waist apron, cargo pants, and keep pricing simple.

A 3-pocket waist apron can speed up making change by keeping change right in front of you. The main pocket of the apron should be the home of the ones, fives, and tens. In one of the other pockets, keep quarters, and one of the additional pockets should be used for large bills.

The cargo pants should be for excess cash, pens, phone, or extra items. When pricing your items, keep pricing simple. Everything should be sold in even dollar amounts and offer discounts on multiple items based on fives or tens.

Best Practice 5: Build Connections. At any farmers market, some vendors have people who always buy from them. These relationships take time to develop, but these bonds provide a steady supply of loyal customers. These connections can become customers who will visit your farm and become part of your farm's community.

Best Practice 6: Cooperation over Competition. A good farmers market will be a community of growers. In some markets, there is a second market at the end of the day where people share and trade leftovers. At the very best markets, there are no leftovers, and vendors just swap stories.

Best Practice 7: Customer Centered. Put yourself in the place of your customer. *Your customer's experience builds the perception of your farm.* The customer experience includes displays, quality products, and human interaction.

Greet people! Stand and be ready to say hello or mention the beautiful heirloom tomatoes you have for sale. Do not sit in a chair and stare at your phone – unless you do not want to make many sales that day.

Best Practice 8: Illusion of Abundance. Displays need to be overflowing and inviting. Keep displays stacked or at an angle to keep produce visually appealing. Use smaller boxes as larger boxes become empty. Mix and match produce to keep tables and boxes full. Remember the adage *stack it high and watch it fly.*

Best Practice 9: Avoid Ambiguities. Clearly state prices along with vegetable names, types, and other relevant details. Some farmers use clothespins attached to baskets with prices. Chalkboards with colorful chalks are popular with many vendors. Others write directly on baskets or buckets. Keep in mind, many customers will move to the next vendor before asking about price.

Best Practice 10: Merchandise Effectively. Market savvy farmers include their logo on everything and everywhere possible. The internet makes it easy to purchase a canopy with the farm's logo. Also, invest in vehicle magnets, clothing, hats, and other specialty products with your farm logo.

Best Practice 11: Visual Appeal. Color moves farm products, and colorful displays attract attention. Bright yellow, green, and orange colors communicate freshness, taste, and overall quality. Always use contrasting colors to maximize visual appeal. Lastly, an attractive visual appeal is best achieved by keeping your stand tidy and organized.

Best Practice 12: Learn. Always be on the lookout for great ideas. At any farmers market, someone will be doing something that you can either copy or improve upon. Analyze what other people do well and what they do not do well, and most importantly, what you can learn from them.

Best Practice 13: Greet First; Sell Second. At every farmers market, there are hard sellers, and there are chair sitters. Neither extreme is useful. *The best option is to be an active seller.* Active sellers engage people by acknowledging them and allowing natural conversations to develop.

Best Practice 14: DIY Marketing. Remember, your farm is your business, and no one cares more about your business than you do. The job of the farmers market manager is to promote the farmers market. While the manager may highlight vendors, it is not the manager's job to advocate your farm. Do your own marketing and let your customers know what markets you are attending and when.

Best Practice 15: Provide Samples. Providing samples shows confidence in your product. It also allows people to "test drive" your products before they buy. A friendly and engaging farmer providing samples to customers is the apex of the customer's experience at any farmers market.

The University of Kentucky conducted market research on the effects of sampling at a farmers market and found the following:

- 55% of people who purchased a product said they did not intend to buy the product, but the sample convinced them to buy the product.
- 96% of people who sample items at a farmers market have a positive experience of that sample.
- 45% of people who taste a product purchase a product.
- 34% of people who sampled a product recommend the product to a friend.
- Free samples increase sales more than any other strategy.

If you are not offering samples at the farmers market, you should be. This gesture will build your customer base and profitability.

Best Practice 16: Provide Recipes. This gives customers a tool for how to use your products. Recipes spark interest, increase anticipation, and give customers a reason to buy your products. These recipes need to include your farm's logo, social media information, website, and contact information. It is worth noting that most vendors do not provide recipes. Being the vendor who does offer them is a great way to set yourself apart from the crowded marketplace.

Best Practice 17: Listen to Customers. This is the best form of market research. Many customers will talk their way through their purchases, letting you know what they are purchasing and why. This is an opportunity to think about new products to produce, make recommendations, or give suggestions. Most importantly, *listening to customers communicates caring.*

Best Practice 18: Price with Pride. Think about how Starbucks prices its coffee, and price your produce the same way. A general rule of thumb is to visit higher-end grocery stores and price your products according to their higher prices for similar products.

Slightly higher than market prices signal quality. Use price as a signal of product supremacy and deliver on that higher quality. Remember, it is always easier to lower prices than to raise prices. Higher prices also allow for price discounts on bulk purchases.

Best Practice 19: Proper Packaging. Packaging helps create brand loyalty, and a well-designed package communicates quality. Proper packaging helps with transaction times. Prepackaged products reduce handling time at market, allowing you to serve more customers.

The packaging is an extension of your brand. People buy with their eyes. Proper packaging appeals to a customer's eyes and feels pleasant to the touch. We have all purchased a product based on its package, and your customers are no different.

Best Practice 20: Develop a "Twitter Response." Explain in just a few sentences on why and how you farm. In the farm to table world, people are more concerned about why you farm and how you farm than what you farm. There is no need to give a dissertation; offer a brief summary that takes seconds to explain. This is the modern version of the traditional elevator pitch and should last no longer than a short elevator ride of 20 to 30 seconds.

Conclusion

Farmers markets offer many benefits for small farmers. These are great places to start building your business, finding customers, and building your brand. Just keep in mind that the marketplace can be crowded, and you will need to work to set yourself apart! If a market is not working for you, find another one.

Small Farm Marketing Strategy 11: Farm Stand & Farm Store (start here)

"Understanding where your food comes from, trying to bolster local farmers and local economies, and having a better connection to the food around you and the people around you, only good can come of that." ~ Amos Lee

Farm stores and farm stands can do well just about anywhere. They do exceptionally well if you are near a large town or city. However, even if you live in the middle of nowhere, you can still do well-selling products off your farm. In my little area, multiple families are making a living selling farm products off their farm. Having a farm store is one of my favorite marketing methods.

Ten reasons to sell products on your farm:

1. **Fixed costs.** It is not going to cost you any more to sell your products where you grow products. Some farmers start with a farmers market style booth, sell out of a barn, or under a shade tree.

2. **Simple and Scalable.** A farm store can be as simple as a shade tree (an Amish neighbor started his store under a shade tree). From this humble beginning, you can add to your store and grow the business.

3. **Transparency.** People can visually verify you do what you say you do the way you claim to do it. This allows you to tell people you are "customer certified." When people visit your farm store and see your operation in action, it endears them to your farm.

   This also does away with the need for third-party certifications. The reason people ask about these endorsements is to provide verification of your farm's practices - but if your visitor is on-site, they can see your operation for themselves. A farm store offers the ultimate in farm transparency.

4. **Engagement.** Customers enjoy buying from the source. In today's world, most people, even in rural settings, do not have the opportunity to visit a working farm.

   People would much rather visit a small farm than a big box store. Small farms provide a rich sensory experience. Even the unpleasant smells offer a sense of authenticity that is missing in today's over-merchandised shopping experience.

5. **Convenient.** Being open during the week allows people the freedom to buy local food without getting up early on Saturday. Being open multiple days of the week provides more opportunities for people to spend money with you.

6. **Less Competition**. Instead of setting up at an already crowded farmers market, you are the only person selling at this venue. Instead of marketing to stores or restaurants who have current relationships with other farmers, you are making connections with people who are willing to pay full retail for your product – right off your farm.

7. **More Attention**. You have the customer's full attention. When a person visits your farm store, take advantage of this by working to build a relationship. This increased attention keeps the customer's focus on your farm, which is where you want the customer's focus to be.

8. **Your Rules**. Every farmers market has rules, and many of these rules just do not make sense. Most farmers markets are brought into existence as the result of committee meetings with people who decided that a given location would be a good location for a farmers market. Rules set up by a committee are designed for lawsuit protection and prevention – they are not there for the interest of the vendor. When you start a farm store, it is your store and your rules.

9. **Your Business**. A farm store is your business. Either it can stay a small business supplementing a current income, or it can be something nurtured and grown into a full-time income.

10. **Control**. A farm store allows you freedom. You set the hours whereas a farmers market dictates when you must arrive and when you can leave. It is a waste of time and frustratng to be stuck at a market after selling out because you are waiting for permission to leave. Something that does happen.

With your store, if you sell out, you are free to do other tasks. When business is slow, you are free to work on other tasks between customers. The control you get from owning a farm store provides you the freedom to live life by your rules: not someone else's.

Best Practices for Small Farms: Farm Store

Best Practice 1: Visibility. People should see your farm store as soon as they arrive on your property. If possible, it needs to be close to your main road. If this is not possible, there must be clear directions to the store. If you have multiple buildings, label the store clearly.

Best Practice 2: Merchandising. Displaying your products is imperative. Proper merchandising plays a huge role in getting people to buy anything. Treat your farm store with the same marketing shrewdness that grocery stores treat their business. Here are six merchandising tips:

1. **Fresh**. People are not driving to a farm to get old products. Make sure all products are fresh and ready to eat. Create a "bargain bin" for old products, or better yet manufacture these old products into new, value-added products.

2. **Clean**. Small farms are dirty, but your store shouldn't be. Keep it orderly, tidy, and organized. Wipe the dirt off your produce. Imperfect produce is acceptable and trending among localvores. Many organic or naturally grown customers actively look for imperfect produce as evidence of preferred growing practices.

3. **Bursting Displays**. Display bins and trays need to be full. Full shelves are a sign of a well-run business. People like to buy out of abundance. This also allows people to pick the product they desire, making them feel as if they got a great deal.

4. **Rotate stock.** FIFO is the practice of making sure the first item in is the first item out. Proper stock rotation ensures that your best products are always out front and ready for the customer's enjoyment.

5. **Cross merchandise**. Mix and match produce or products with items that go well together to make a meal. This will increase sales while providing a higher level of service.

6. **Point of Purchase (POP) Marketing**. Provide recipe cards, growing information, or sustainability efforts with different items to increase awareness.

Best Practice 3: Customer Loyalty Program. This communicates to customers you care about them. This can be as simple as a punch card that people redeem for an item or discount, or it can be a complicated database used to track buying habits. The goal of this program is to communicate to customers that you appreciate their business.

Best Practice 4: Events and Demonstrations. This is an agritourism approach to your farm store. There are many events you could host at your farm that people will find attractive. Here is a partial list of ideas:

- Cooking
- Food storing
- Holiday events
- Watermelon eating
- Winemaking
- Pumpkin carving
- Sauce making
- Bee Keeping
- Baking

Best Practice 5: Freebies. This could be as simple as giving balloons to kids or promotional items with your farm's name to customers. If your farm is mission-driven, consider giving away tree saplings cloned from trees from your farm, seeds, or plants. People like free stuff and free things can give people a reason to talk about you.

Best Practice 6: Signage. A business with no sign is a sign of no business. Your farm store needs a sign that clearly identifies it as a store. Your displays need to have clear signage that explains what an item is, what it costs, how it is sold (per piece, pound, box, etc.), and price.

Best Practice 7: Organize. There needs to be a linear or logical flow to your store and displays. Visit grocery stores, farm stores, or similar retail outlets and make notes of how those stores are laid out, and learn from these people.

Best Practice 8: Consistent Hours. People need to know when you are open. It is fine not to be open all day every day, but store hours must be consistent. They also need to be convenient for your customers. If store hours are 9 to 5, working people with those same hours are not going to visit. If you want an eight-hour day, try 11 to 7. This allows customers to shop after they get off from work on their way home while giving you time to run errands before the store opens, or to get the store ready for the day.

Best Practice 9: Package Deals. Mix and match products so that you can offer package deals for your customers. This will help sell more products.

Best Practice 10: Business Card Drawings. Have a fishbowl for people to drop their card in for a chance at a prize. This is a great way to build a customer contact list.

Best Practice 11: Group Discounts. By offering discounts to groups such as the military, first responders, teachers, large employers, non-profits, and churches, you are giving large groups of people reasons to buy from you with little marketing effort.

Best Practice 12: Parking. There needs to be a designated parking area. This area does not need paving, but it needs to be clearly marked along with clear directions for the flow of traffic.

Best Practice 13: Play Area. Have an area where kids can play old-time games such as horseshoes, beanbag tosses, tire swings, etc. This will keep kids occupied, giving parents more time to shop for bigger purchases.

Best Practice 14: Customer Service. Speak to everyone who enters your store. These people are the reason you are farming and not an interruption to your day. Be excited that people have chosen to visit your store even if they are just looking. If you make them feel welcomed, they will be more likely to return as a customer.

Best Practice 15: Marketing. People need to know about your farm store. Market your store along with your products and farm. Use the strategies in this book to build traffic to your farm store. Farm stores do not succeed without effort – they require diligent marketing efforts.

Conclusion

A farm store gives you more control over selling your farm products. With a farm store, you are free to set the policies, hours, products, and prices. Farm stores flourish almost everywhere and can actually become a family destination. Granted, people may not drive miles for a piece of squash or a single turnip, but people will drive for miles for an experience; therefore, make your farm store an adventure.

Small Farm Internet Marketing: 10 Proven Strategies

"Our philosophy is - using internet technology, we can make every company become Amazon." ~ *Jack Ma*

Small farms need to be using the internet, especially social media. The internet has changed the competitive landscape by making it easier for small farms to compete with larger, established corporations. Tech companies such as eBay, Google, or Amazon all started as an idea with no tangible product; today, they are giants.

Companies such as Omaha Steaks, Misfit Market, Blue Apron, Salsa Basket, and many others use the internet to sell farm-related products. These competitors are using technology to gain your customers, and you should be using technology to fight back.

The internet offers a low-cost way of reaching local customers while giving your farm a global presence. For a small farm, social media such as Facebook or Instagram provides tools for community building. It takes intention, purpose, and commitment to build this community; however, this community is your best protection against larger multinational companies who want to put you out of business.

Seven Social Media Guidelines for Small Farms

- **Relevance**. Be relevant to your customer's wants and needs.
- **Avoid Politics**. Your social media should not be a political platform but a business and community building platform.
- **Responsive**. When people send a message, respond within a few hours, and always respond within a day.
- **Constant Contact**. For best results post a few times a week but not several times a day.
- **Schedule**. Use the tools on the platform to schedule your postings.
- **Quality Followers (or likes).** It is better to have a smaller presence of people who are actually going to buy from you than a large fan base of non-customers.
- **Experiment**. It is crucial to grow your online presence. Be on the lookout for new platforms and platforms that resonate with your target market.

Small Farm Internet Marketing Strategy 1: Farm Website

"When we launched the Wine Library website in 1996, I didn't even own a computer yet. I just understood that there was an opportunity here to market differently."
~ Gary Vaynerchuk

In today's world, a website is required for anyone running a business. It has been said, *"A business with no sign is a sign of no business."* Today's version of a sign is a website.

Websites are great for farm products. I get new customers all the time through my site; it has more than paid for itself, and it will continue to pay for itself. With the ease of technology, anyone who can use a smartphone or log on to the internet can build a website, and many hosting companies provide inexpensive templates.

In the early days of the internet, websites required knowledge of coding, HTML and other specialized skills. Early on, sites were out of reach of the average small farmer. That is no longer the case. Today there are hundreds of low-cost web hosting providers with easy to use templates. Here are just a few providers:

- Wix.com
- Myhosting.com
- Bluehost.com
- Siteground.com
- Godaddy.com
- Squareup.com
- Squarespace.com
- Weebly.com

- Shopify.com
- Jimdo.com
- Duda.com
- GoCentral.com
- WordPress.com
- IMCreator.com
- EzyWebs.com

Each provider has different benefits, features, and prices, and you should research these providers to find one that feels right for your farm.

Ten Website Benefits for Small Farms

1. Local Connection. Google, Facebook, and many other websites offer local recommendations. When people search for local farm products, having a website allows these people to find you, and it will enable these people to learn more about your farm.

2. Customer Expectations. People expect all businesses to have a website. Many customers use sites as a source of information that details products, services, contact information, hours, and other relevant information.

3. Efficiency. A website is a timesaving device, and many people would prefer to visiting a website than make a phone call. These fewer calls reduce daily interruptions while allowing more people to get information about your farm and allowing you to get more farm work accomplished. These days, some people simply will not call. If you don't meet their expectation of having a website, you will instantly lose them as a customer.

4. Reviews and Recommendations. Your website is a great place to post customer testimonies. The best thing about reviews on your website is you control the content.

5. National Reach. The entire country is open for business with a website. If you sell jams, jellies, wines, frozen meat, hatching eggs, day-old chicks, or other legally shippable items, your customer base is the entire country. There may be legal restrictions for some products, and the local post office can answer shipping questions.

6. Content Control. With your own website, you can say whatever you want the way you want to say it. You control the pictures and images, and most importantly, you control the message.

7. Around-the-Clock Ordering. A farm website allows you to take orders all day, every day. A website is like a dedicated employee who never sleeps, calls in sick, or takes the day off.

8. Farmhand Resource. Your website should provide all the information a farmhand needs to answer customer questions.

9. Credibility. A website is evidence of competence and professionalism. Having your vision/mission statements on your site with your farm values gives new customers greater faith in your farm.

10. Customer Information Harvest. A website is a great way to collect information and to build a distribution list by asking people to share their contact information.

When creating a website from scratch or with a template, here are thirteen best practices every farm website should follow.

Best Practices for Small Farms: Farm Website

Best Practice 1: Domain Name. Own your domain name. You need to register the domain name directly with the hosting provider. Do not let anyone else do this for you. It gives that person control over your farm's name and online presence. A domain should be unique, and if your farm's name is not available as a domain name, you may want to rethink your farm's name.

Best Practice 2: Guiding Principles. This page is for your farm's vision and mission statement, along with your farm values. This communicates why you do what you do and what your farm stands for.

Best Practice 3: About Us Page. This page allows you to tell your farm story. This page makes you a real person to your customers. The About Us page should include a picture of the people, products, and farm.

Best Practice 4: Products and Services. This page gives information about what products are in season and their prices. This page needs to include your services as well.

Best Practice 5: FAQ. These are common questions that you get asked all of the time. This section is a great place to give your farm personality. You can put fun facts in there or be playful with your information. It's also the place to put the questions you get tired of answering. People will still ask, however, not as many people.

Best Practice 6: Social Media Handles. Small farms need to engage with customers through as many channels as possible. Many people live by or through their social media accounts. When they follow you on social media, it creates a personal relationship.

Best Practice 7: Contact Information. Your website must include your address, phone number, and email. It is a great business strategy to make it easy for people to contact you and to buy from you.

Best Practice 8: CSA. If you operate a CSA, this needs inclusion on the website. Ideally, people will be able to subscribe to the CSA online. This page requires to include the guidelines, drop off locations, products included, and other information about the program.

Best Practice 9: Blog. Blogging is a great marketing tool. It allows you to keep in touch with customers. Your blog should have a page on your website. If the two aren't connected, make sure you include a link.

Best Practice 10: Press Releases. These are stories that you have sent to the local media. Having a list of press releases on your website makes it easy for media to research your farm.

Best Practice 11: Press Kit. A press kit provides general information about your farm for the media to use. Please refer to the chapter in this book for more information on Press Kits.

Best Practice 12: Store. If you have products for sale, your website is a great place to sell your farm products. Your online store can also include items such as farm merchandise (T-shirts, gift cards, coffee mugs, etc.). While it is excellent if you have these products on hand to sell, keep in mind there are on-demand printing places online, such as cafepress.com, that will house your logo and print as things are purchased.

Best Practice 13: E-brochure. Hard-copy brochures are expensive to design and print. Save money by creating a PDF version available for download via your website. There is definitely some crossover with e-brochures and the information sheets mentioned in the Small Farm PR Chapter on creating a Press Kit. Tweak an information sheet, and you will have an E-brochure!

Conclusion

A website is a foundation for any online marketing activity. Once a site is developed, it is easy to update and maintain. If you do not have a website, get one. A useful website does not necessarily need to be fancy or flashy. A basic template can accomplish a great deal and is much better than nothing.

Small Farm Internet Marketing Strategy 2: Farm Blogging

"Don't focus on having a great blog. Focus on producing a blog that's great for your readers." ~ **Brian Clark.**

A blog is an online journal chronicling your farm adventure. People follow blogs for many reasons: staying connected, pursuing interests, or for education. Using blogs as a marketing tool helps to make and maintain connections by building relationships with people interested in your farm. Blogs do more than promote products; blogs forge relationships and interest in you and your farm.

Nine Benefits of Small Farm Blogging.

1. **Loyalty**. People reading blogs tend to be committed to the person or organization producing the blog. Blogging allows your farm story to "season" with readers. By season, I mean developing a deep connection to your farm through the sharing of stories over a long period.
2. **Control**. Writing a blog allows you to control the story because you write the story. A blog is an opportunity to talk methodically about your beliefs, passions, and practices. A blog gives voice to your farm.
3. **Community**. Blogs allow customers to feel as if they are part of a community. Many blogs allow people to comment and participate in a discussion, which can build rapport with new people.

4. **Economical**. Blogs are cost effective. There are many free or low-cost blog providers.
5. **Search placement**. Blogs improve search engine placement. Search engine indexing uses the number of links to a website to determine that website's placement in search results. The more linking to a blog or website, the better the search rankings for that blog or website.
6. **Authority**. Blogs establish you as a leader and expert in the farm community. In any industry, being a leader is always a great business practice. By sharing your opinions, knowledge, and experience, you are letting the world know you know something.
7. **Viral**. Blogs can go viral. You may blog on a topic that touches people in such a way that they want to share it with friends and family. When a blog post goes viral, it exposes your farm to people who otherwise would never know about you or your farm. You can never guarantee or know if this might happen, but if it does, it means excellent exposure.
8. **Fresh**. Blogs are a source of fresh, new content to your website. Regular blogging keeps your internet presence lively, active and engaged.
9. **Simple**. Blogs are easy to start, maintain, and operate. If you can type, you can blog by using one of the internet's easy to use templates.

Many websites offer free or low-cost blogging tools. As of this writing, here are a few blogging sources:

- Wordpress.org
- Wix.com
- Medium.com
- Ghost.com
- Blogger.com
- Weebly.com

- Joomla.org
- Squarespace.com

This list is subject to change, and a quick internet search will provide a list of blogging websites. The best place to host a blog is your website. Free sites have limitations, but more importantly, using your website to host a blog encourages visitors to your website instead of a tech company's website.

Best Practices for Small Farms: Blogging

Best Practice 1: Grammar. Grammar is essential for blogs. A common mistake is to write as you speak. Many people think this is conversational; however, it usually just jumbled and rambling. The best blogs are professionally written but have a conversational tone.

Best Practice 2: Audience Interest. A farm blog with no readers is useless. It is essential to write blogs that appeal to customers' interests. Possible topics for a farm blog include recipes, farming practices, chores, canning, animal stories, news, and other how-to entries. Don't forget to write about things going wrong – this makes you real to people and can be the best at conveying the hard work you do.

Best Practice 3: Consistency. A regularly published blog gets more subscribers. Research shows the more businesses blog, the more people subscribe. The optimal blog post number is twice a week; according to blogging research, this increases subscribers 18% faster than monthly blogging.

Best Practice 4: Use Your Voice. Chris Pirillo, founder and CEO of LockerGnome gives this advice, *"Stay true to yourself and your voice. People don't care to follow sites so much as they care to follow people."* Let your personality shine through your blog, and use your blog to share your passion and farm's mission.

Best Practice 5: Persistence. It takes time to develop a following. For blogging to be effective and for the audience to grow, it will take time. As with many endeavors, the most successful people are the people who have worked at it the longest.

Best Practice 6: Fine-Tuning. As you blog, pay attention to what works and what does not. Treat failure as a learning opportunity and not a reason to quit.

Best Practice 7: Hook 'Em. Catchy headlines are imperative for increasing blog readership. Focus on developing hooks that give people a reason to read and subscribe to your blog. Soundbites drive media, so use them when developing headlines. Blog headlines must grab a person's attention and draw people into the blog.

Best Practice 8: The 2S model. Short and straightforward blogs are the most popular with the average word count being between 300 to 1,000 words. This is just 3 – 5 paragraphs, which would include an introduction, body, and conclusion.

Best Practice 9: Be Authentic. Be honest and share the good and the bad. Blog readers want to connect with the real you and not some pretentious version of yourself that supports an unrealistic social expectation.

Best Practice 10: Be Resilient. The naysayers will be vocal, and your most loyal readers will be silent. People will post rude comments and shred your work. Delete and ban these people; do not engage them.

Best Practice 11: Set Goals. Goals provide motivation and benchmarks to keep progress on target and on track. Set a goal for the number of articles or number of subscribers you are working toward. Remember, without a goal, not much happens.

Best Practice 12: Be Strategic. Develop new content, focus on your brand, and be relevant. Treat blogging like a microbusiness that supports your farm.

Best Practice 13: Guest Blog. Share your blogs with other bloggers. This will expose your blog to people who would not otherwise get an opportunity to read your blog or to learn about your farm. Also, use guest bloggers. This provides a mutual benefit for both parties.

Best Practice 14: Get Started. Just do it. The first several blog entries do not need to be great. Each blog post gets more natural and enjoyable as you develop them. The key to blogging is to do something even if it is terrible. Pick a topic or blog title and write something, and then revise it as needed.

Conclusion

Blogging gives voice to your passion and builds your farm's brand. There are many easy to use and free blogging tools to get you started.

Small Farm Internet Marketing Strategy 3: Google Business (Local)

"Google, the internet world, the internet power, and the internet advantages, where, there, all the monopolies die and disappear, and the talent is visible to the globe." ~ *Ehsan Sehgal*

Google Business allows you some control over what people see when they use Google to search for your farm. This is a free, easy to use service from Google. Google's business and reputation depend on accurate information; therefore, your information helps Google stay profitable. Also, Google will offer to sell you keywords, so this "free service" builds Google's sales pipeline.

If you can use Gmail, you can use Google Business by logging into Google Business using your Gmail account. To get the most out of Google Business, follow these best practices.

Six Best Google Business Practices for Small Farms

Best Practice 1: Verify. If you do not verify your farm as your business, Google will depend upon other people's input. This is problematic. People can and will give inaccurate information - sometimes by mistake and sometimes on purpose. Google is such a dominant force in the marketplace that you want to make sure the information they share about your farm is correct.

Verifying a farm as your business is quite easy. Log into Google Business using your Gmail account (you must use Gmail for this) and click a button that says verify. Google will send you a postcard with a secret code for you to enter. This code claims your farm as your business.

If your farm is not listed, you can add your farm to Google by clicking the "add location" button and following the prompts. Once again, to verify your farm, Google will send a postcard with a secret code.

Best Practice 2: Profile Management. When Google has verified your farm, you can manage your farm's profile on Google. This allows you to post hours, respond to reviews, make comments, add a website, and add photos; this puts your farm on Google maps.

Best Practice 3: Images. Google allows you to post pictures. This is a great place to post photos of your farm, products, and logo. There is no need to update the images with the same frequency you do with social media, but the pictures need to build your farm's brand and convey your farm's story.

Best Practice 4: Respond to Reviews. Google allows you to respond to customer reviews. A good practice is to respond to all reviews, good or bad. If you do get a bad review, respond, and offer to make it better.

Best Practice 5: Questions and Answers. Answering questions on Google can reduce phone calls and cut down on unnecessary interruptions. When answering questions, always refer people to your website, social media platforms, or encourage them to call if they have more questions.

Best Practice 6: Make Updates and Posts. Google Business allows for posts. This is an excellent place to make event announcements, let people know what products are in season, holiday closings, or other relevant information.

Conclusion

Google is the most popular search engine; therefore, it just makes sense to manage your farm's profile. People trust Google searches, and given the potential for misinformation, it is vital to control your farm's profile. Managing your profile builds your farm's brand and is another channel for communicating with potential customers.

Small Farm Internet Marketing Strategy 4: Create infographics

"The life of a visual communicator should be one of systematic and exciting intellectual chaos." ~ **Alberto Cairo**

An infographic turns complex information into a simple picture. Infographics have progressed from fad to trend to mainstream use. People share infographics on all social media platforms, texts, websites, and virtually any other form of electronic messaging.

The average social media user is 30 times more likely to read an infographic versus text-only content. Infographics are a cultural fit for today's quick, instant information world. Infographics provide seven marketing benefits:

- People are 40% more responsive to visual information than written information.

- Infographics are easy to share. Users can just copy and paste into websites, blogs, social media, and print.

- Infographics are great tools for recruiting new followers or for creating new social media connections.

- Of all the information processed by the brain, 90% is visual.

- Visual information is processed 600,000 times faster than text.

- Visual cues increase credibility. A study by Wharton School of Business found that when using visual aids, believability increases by 67% even for inaccurate information.

Infographics serve four purposes when used for small farm marketing:

- **Data Simplification.** For example, an infographic may compare the number of chemicals an industrial farm uses compared to what a small farm uses. This can make a rather large and abstract number seem real and concerning.
- **Providing Information.** The most effective infographics are educational. For a mission-driven farm, an infographic visualizes your rationale for your farm's mission or farm practices.
- **Advertorial**. This editorial style infographic promotes a small farm while looking as if it is merely sharing facts.
- **Branding.** An infographic creates a visual expression of a farm's brand.

Best Practices for Small Farms: the Infographic

Best Practice 1: Purpose. Are you trying to promote a specific product, share information, build your brand, or develop a campaign on behalf of a social or environmental issue?

Best Practice 2: Template Selection. Unless you are a graphic artist fluent with Adobe products or other similar software, use a template. Many customizable templates are either cheap or free. Using a template saves time, money, and energy, allowing you to spend time on message development and farm chores.

Best Practice 3: Headline. The headline must capture people's attention. For maximum impact, use a surprising statistic, fact, or trend.

Best Practice 4: Data Verified Decisions. When numbers need explaining, use an infographic to compare sizes and quantities. Pictures give non-math people a tool for making sense of numbers.

Best Practice 5: Straightforward. Infographics depend on images and layout for message communication instead of text. The best practice includes minimal text while sharing only one or two ideas at a time. It is better to create multiple short infographics than one large or long infographic.

Best Practice 6: Linear Progression. The best infographics use a logical pattern. Linear patterns are easy, simple to follow, and comfortable; all of this makes them easily acceptable. This is the beauty and essence of infographics-complex issues can be made concise.

Best Practice 7: Experiment. Try different layouts and templates for your infographic. Keep track of what works and what does not work.

Sources to Create Infographics

Here are five online resources to get started with infographics. This is not even close to an exhaustive list, and a quick internet search will yield many additional websites. Try a few sites and stick with the one that works best for your needs.

- Venngage.com
- Piktochart.com
- Canva.com
- Infogram.com
- Lucidpress.com

Conclusion

A well-crafted infographic clearly communicates your mission, vision, and practices in a sharable, easy to understand format. Because of their shareability and graphic appeal, infographics are an excellent medium for increasing the reach of your farm's message.

Small Farm Internet Marketing Strategy 5: Create a Podcast

*The secret to podcast success is sticking with it and making it fun for yourself. ~ **Lauren Lapkus***

A Podcast is a downloadable talk show that people subscribe to and listen to at their leisure. This feature is one of the driving forces of podcast popularity. Another feature is quality. Quality podcasts focus on a few central issues or topics. Podcasts automatically update. This makes it easy for listeners to stay up to date with their favorite programs and hosts. Podcasts can be daily, weekly, or monthly. Any choice can bring success, but consistency is paramount.

Anyone with a computer or smartphone can create a podcast. There is no need for a studio, expensive equipment, or staff. All you need is your voice, a topic, a place to publish. Podcasts are great marketing tools. Here are eleven reasons you should be podcasting.

- **Brand Voice**. Your customers can hear you talk about your mission, vision, farm practices, and the reasons behind your work. A podcast allows you to share your passion for farming with people who care and people who want to get to know you.

- **Increased Credibility**. People assume you are an expert when your podcast. Whether or not you are an expert is up for debate; however, a marketing axiom states, *"Perception is reality."* Just remember consistent podcasting will turn you into an expert.

- **Commitment Builder**. People who follow your farm on social media and who listen to your podcast will become farm advocates. One thing better than a repeat customer is an advocate. Podcasting creates customer loyalty, making podcasts one of the most effective and convincing forms of advertising.

- **Self-Reflection**. As you develop a podcast, it will be natural to analyze desires, decisions, and direction. Thinking deeply about these three Ds will help guide the small farm journey while making you both a better farmer and a better human.

- **Portability**. The most common place people listen to podcasts is in their car. Podcasting allows people the freedom to consume new information or entrainment according to their schedule.

- **Self-Improvement.** As you develop podcast content, it forces you to learn more about farming, business, or whatever topic you choose. The absolute best way to learn something is to teach it, and a podcast is a teaching forum.

- **Communication Skills**. As you develop and improve your podcast, this skill will automatically transfer to your public speaking and interpersonal communication.

- **Friendly**. A podcast subscriber is entering your world while inviting you into their world. This connection turns you into a real person who goes with them on rides or walks; you are the person they listen to while they work around the house.

- **Inexpensive**. There is not much in the way of cost. If you want to invest in expensive recording equipment, you could, or you could use just a smartphone or computer. There's a middle ground, too. The right equipment can make you sound more professional, and it doesn't have to be the best on the market.

- **Sharable Content.** A podcast is something to share on social media, your website, or an internet radio station.

- **Niche Building**. People who subscribe to a podcast are looking for information about a specific topic/issue.

Best Practices for Small Farms: Podcasts

Best Practice 1: Topic Selection. This is going to drive the podcast. Topic selections start with answering these questions: why do I want to discuss this topic? What is the rationale for podcasting? Is it to attract customers? Is it to learn more about farming? Is it to position yourself as an industry leader? Is it to campaign for a cause? Is it to create an ongoing dialog for a brand story?

Best Practice 2: Title and Subtitle. This is all about marketing. The title and subtitle must spark interest and draw people in to listen. The goal is to develop an apropos title and subtitle that explains the topic.

Best Practice 3. Content. Good content strikes a balance between factual and fascinating storytelling. The best podcast educates by entertaining its listeners. Developing great content is a process requiring revising, rewriting, editing, and reworking.

Best Practice 4. Summary and Description. This is a brief description of your podcast. The best descriptions are direct and immediately get to the point. Tell people who you are, podcast purpose, and what they can expect from the podcast.

Best Practice 5: Logo and Artwork. People are attracted to visuals. If your logo does not look professional, people will not give you or your podcast a chance. When developing the artwork, align it with your farm's brand and logo.

Best Practice 6: Editing. Good editing is the difference between sounding professional or amateurish. Having the right software or mixer makes editing much more manageable. There are digital mixers (or software) that will work great for podcasting for under $100.00.

Best Practice 7: Length. There is not an official time limit for a podcast. However, the average commute time is 25 minutes, and the average podcast is 30 minutes. I think length depends on the topic and your podcasting style. If your shows are filled with good content and flow, people will listen. My best advice is to listen to podcasts, find one you like and think works, and mirror your format off of that one.

Best Practice 8: Consistent Style and Format. People thrive on consistency. Consistently producing a podcast makes it easier for listeners to incorporate it into their routine. Besides, consistency demonstrates that you are credible and serious.

In the beginning, consistency may be difficult. That is okay. You do not have to publish podcasts until you are ready to publish them. Use this development and start-up time to ensure consistency by building a podcast pipeline.

Best Practice 9: Professional Intro. It is more than a cliché to say you only get one chance to make a first impression. You should have professional-sounding music and editing for your podcast. Some companies specialize in producing introductions if you are not comfortable creating it yourself.

Best Practice 10: Sign off Slogan/Phrase. When ending the podcast, have a sign off phrase. There may be slight variations, but a good quality sign-off phrase signals the episode is complete. This will also make your podcast feel more professional and intentional.

Best Practice 11: Be Original. Being true to your views and perceptions is the best way to get people to tune in. The only real competitive advantage, a business, farm, person, or podcast, can maintain is life experiences and story.

Selected Podcast Software

Here is a list of software used by many podcasters. I have not tried all this software, so treat this as just a source for research.

- Zencastr
- Anchor
- Auphonic
- Cleanfeed
- Logic Pro X
- Audacity
- Adobe Audition
- Sony ACID Xpress
- WavePad Audio Editor Software
- Spreaker Studio.

Conclusion

Podcasts are great marketing tools. Podcasting has been around since 2004, and it continues to grow in popularity in terms of listeners and creators. A podcast gives a farm an actual voice and allows listeners to connect with you, your work, and your farm.

Small Farm Internet Marketing Strategy 6: #Marketing

"Hashtag activism is a catalyst, but things have to actually happen in real life." ~ **Petra Collins**

A hashtag (the "#" symbol) is an essential part of social media. Hashtags allow posts or content sharing outside of your network. A hashtag is a simple command that indexes content according to a topic. Once indexed, this content is discoverable by anyone on that platform who uses, searches, or follows that hashtag.

Ten reasons to use hashtags

Reason 1: Free. Hashtags provide free marketing. It gets your message to people who have clearly expressed interest in the topic.

Reason 2: Easy. Adding a hashtag is as easy as typing the # symbol followed by a word or phrase without spaces, for example, #smallfarm, and the highlighted text is now a hashtag.

Reason 3: Audience development. Hashtags increase the number of people who can see and interact with your content.

Reason 4: Increased Followers or Likes. Exposing content to a wider audience increases the number of new people who will want to hear from you again.

Reason 5: Attention-Getting. A proper hashtag can get people to read your content.

Reason 6: Opportunity. Hashtags create connections to existing stories. Placing a hashtag on a story about a lettuce or spinach recall is an opportunity to connect your farm to people who are looking for a local source of safe food. You can also comment on stories with relevant hashtags and your farm's hashtag. You want to be intentional with it, but when done well, it can increase your presence on social media.

Reason 7: Engagement. Hashtags build engagement with people who are actually interested in your farm's mission. Hashtags are great conversation starters, and this conservation can become an invitation for people to follow your profile, learn about your farm, and buy your products.

Reason 8: Generate Buzz. People like contests. Using hashtags to promote a competition, raffle or promotion is a great tool to encourage people to share your farm's profile. Many users are more likely to retweet hashtags if they know they might win something.

Reason 9: Increased Reach. Hashtags increase comments or reach. Comments or posts with hashtags repeat more than comments or posts without hashtags. Depending on the platform, hashtagged content repeats two or three times more than content without hashtags.

Reason 10: Perception. Proper hashtags can make a farm trendy and cutting edge while positioning it as an industry leader.

Seven Types of Hashtags

Content Hashtags. These hashtags relate to content topics. This hashtag summarizes your posts into a few words or phrases. For a small farm, it may be #locallygrown, #mytowngrown, #grassfed, etc.

Trending hashtags. Trending hashtags are the flavor of the moment. These hashtags may be fun to play and experiment with but may not lead to effective small farm marketing.

All social media platforms have a list of trending hashtags. These hashtags provide a great source of new hashtag ideas; however, these hashtags can drown your message in an ocean of hashtags.

Brand Hashtags. These hashtags build on a farm's brand. Using a farm's name or tagline is always a great marketing idea. If your farm's name is common, choose a different hashtag name, and maybe consider a new farm name. This hashtag needs to be short, simple, and easily spelled.

Product Hashtags. People looking for specific farm products will search using those product names, and hashtags put you in touch with this crowd.

Event Hashtags. This hashtag promotes a specific event and is a useful marketing tool for small farms that host events. This hashtag puts the event in front of interested people. It also gives people who attended the event a chance to post photos or content and properly tag them.

Social Issue Hashtags. People concerned about causes or social issues use hashtags to stay current on those issues. This group contains people who are worried about the environmental impact of large industrial farms, buying locally, or using locally sourced products. This subset will be interested in small farms, and hashtags can put small farms in clear view of this audience.

Local or Location Hashtags. For small farms, searching for local people can be an essential hashtag. While it may not generate as many likes or followers as other hashtags, the new likes or followers are from people more likely to purchase your products.

The Four-Step Hashtag. A hashtag is simple; just follow these four steps:

- **# Symbol.** The "#" is an indexing symbol. Its sole job is to activate the indexing function on social media platforms for comments/post categorization.
- **No Spaces**. Social media platforms use all the letters and numbers following the "#" for indexing. No spaces allowed! Type hashtags with multiple words or phrases as one long word. Example: #itsbeenalongday
- **No punctuation.** The only permitted symbol is the "#" symbol. Also, a number only hashtag is not indexable. Hashtags with numbers must include at least one letter.
- **Flexibility**. Hashtags can be a word, an abbreviation, an acronym, brand name, an invented combination of letters and numbers, or a phrase.

Best Practices for Small Farms: Hashtags

Best Practice 1: Strategic Hashtags. Hashtags must be strategic. On most platforms, a few hashtags are better than many hashtags. People will try to add every possible hashtag for a post, but that strategy often backfires while reducing content engagement. This is because many hashtaggers are serious social media users who guard the integrity of their "hashtags" by marking content as "don't show for this hashtag" or as "spam."

Best Practice 2: Locally Grown and Farm to Table Hashtags. Hashtag content as locally grown and locally sourced to connect with people who are interested in those topics. The best practice is to include the area's name to the hashtag to increase the relevance.

Small farms dependent upon local customers need to use hashtags to connect their farm with people interested in locally grown and farm to table farms. Examples of this include #Springfeildgrown, #Flordiaraised, #Ozarkraised, #Rockymoutainmeat, #Portlandproduced, etc.

Best Practice 3: Popular Hashtags. Use popular hashtags directly related to your farm's products. Popular hashtags extend content reach without being spammy. Think local when looking for popular hashtags. Locally popular hashtags are the absolute best hashtags for small farm marketing.

Best Practice 4: Avoid Hidden Messages. Try to avoid accidentally connecting your farm with an offensive or nefarious movement or trend. Also, when combining multiple words, make sure it does not spell something undesirable or questionable. You want your farm to trend, but you want it to trend for the right reason. When in doubt, search the platform or internet using the hashtag you plan to use. If you make this mistake, delete it, learn from it, and move forward.

Best Practice 5: Save Hashtags. When using the same hashtags for multiple posts, save them as a note on the social networks platform or software being used to manage social media accounts. This saves time while improving brand consistency.

Best Practice 6: Build Brand Specific Hashtags. Develop unique, dedicated, and original brand-specific hashtags. The best practice to make sure others are not using this hashtag is to search using that hashtag. For best results, use a short slogan, quote, or tagline.

Best Practice 7: Invent Hashtags. Do not limit yourself by mimicking other people. Hashtags can be a creative expression for advertising events, promotions, campaigns, or products. Include these creative hashtags in all promotional materials. Lastly, make these hashtags useful, concise, and consistent across social media platforms.

Best Practice 8: Be Conversation Specific. When using a hashtag to join a conversation, that hashtag must be topic-specific, relevant to the topic, and related to your farm. If you are talking about sustainability, instead of using #sustainability use #compost or something more closely related to the subject, or something that summarizes your contribution to the conversation.

Best Practice 9: Start Specific Conservations. This practice is different than the previous practice. The earlier practice was joining related conservations. This practice is initiating conversations, conversations explicitly with people interested in locally grown food, local farm practices, local farmers.

Best Practice 10: Community Awareness. Good businesses know what is happening in their local community. Social media spreads the word about local issues or causes. Being aware allows you to lend assistance when needed. These goodwill gestures are good for the community as well as for your farm.

Every community has bloggers, news media personalities, and activists. Follow these people, join the conservation, and respond when it directly relates to your farm or its mission. This will allow you to promote your farm without sounding as if you are promoting your farm.

Best Practice 11: Simple Hashtags. Complicated hashtags are less useful, harder to read, and easier to misspell. A complicated hashtag is more likely to have a typo causing your message to be lost. There is no need to use the hashtag twice in any content. The hashtag is for indexing and not for emphasis, although some people will use it for attention or as a headline.

Best Practice 12: Give Context. A message that consists only of a hashtag misses an opportunity for context and meaningful content. If you are announcing that tomatoes are ready, don't just send out #tomatoes or #blt. Try sending out "It's BLT season! We have fresh tomatoes at the farm Monday – Saturday from 7:00 a.m. to 4:00 p.m. Call us at 555-555-5555 or visit us at YourFarm.com" #farmfreshblt #farmfreshtomato.

Best Practice 13: Research. Research your hashtag. For small farms, hashtags with under 100 users are too narrow, and hashtags with over 10,000 users are too broad. The best practice is to keep your hashtag local while reaching as many people as you can. Having said that, some narrow hashtags draw interested followers because they hit a niche of some kind.

Best Practice 14: Limit hashtags. According to market research, social media posts with the following number of hashtags received subsequent interactions:

- 1 or 2 hashtags averaged 593 interactions
- 3 to 5 hashtags averaged 416 interactions
- 6 to 10 hashtags averaged 307 interactions
- 10 or more averaged 188 interactions

There were two platform exceptions: Instagram and Pinterest. When using these two platforms, interactions increased as the number of *relevant* hashtags increased.

Conclusion

Hashtags are indexing functions that can put social media content in front of a wider audience. Many people do not understand them and avoid using them, but hashtags are simple to use once you know how they work. Use them to connect with more people who need to know about your farm.

Small Farm Internet Marketing Strategy 7: Twitter

"I particularly like Twitter, because it's short and can be very funny and informative. It's a little bit like having your own radio program." ~ **Margaret Atwood**

Twitter's social media platform allows users to share brief messages called tweets. These short messages are under 280 characters in length and come in many forms: text, pictures, infographics, videos, or hyperlinks to websites, or other social media platforms.

Twitter is simple and easy to use. This social media platform works by allowing people to follow profiles of people, businesses, and organizations. When a profile is followed, the follower can read, reply to, and retweet (share) that person's tweets with their own followers.

For marketing purposes, it is important to have followers. Following people will get people to follow you back. This may get new followers, but whether these followers are going to be customers will be a different story. The best followers are organic followers, and here are five proven strategies to increase the number of organic followers:

- **Reply to tweets.** Replying to tweets gets your tweet in front of the followers of the original tweet, which opens your tweet to new audiences.
- **Clever and concise content.** Getting content retweeted pushes your message out to people who otherwise would not have seen your tweet and now can follow your profile.

- **Consistency**. Tweeting frequently increases the number of opportunities for new follower engagement. It never hurts to tweet the same offer, or other content more than once over a few days.
- **Hashtags**. Twitter runs on hashtags. Proper hashtag use puts content in front of people who are interested in that style of content. Hashtags are a gateway for increased followers, which builds your farm's online presence along with real-life profits.
- **Visual**. Make the content visually appealing. Images and videos garner the most retweets. The two best images for farm tweets are candid farm pictures and infographics showing the benefits of locally sourced food, your farm practices, or product benefits.

Getting started with Twitter. It is easy to get started with Twitter; just follow these three steps to get the most out of Twitter:

Step 1: Profile Creation. This informs the world who you are and why you farm. When creating a small farm profile, focus on the farm's brand story and image as you complete the five parts of the twitter profile, which include:

1. **Profile name (handle).** This needs to be the farm's name or a very close version. Twitter handles start with the "@ "symbol followed by up to 15 characters. For example, @ozarkfamilyfarm.
2. **Profile pic.** Choose a photo or image that visually represents your farm. A farm logo is always a great idea. This image will be on every tweet.

3. **Your bio.** This 160-character section describes your farm. When creating this section, include farm location, hours, contact information, products, and a website link.
4. **Header image.** Twitter calls this a "Twitter billboard." Use this section for farm images, product photos, promotions, etc. Changing these images regularly keeps things fresh and dynamic.
5. **Pinned Tweets.** These tweets dwell at the top of a profile. This is the vital information that people need to see when they visit your profile. For a small farm, consider hours, products, and web address.

Step 2: Following. The goal of Twitter, for a small farm, is to attract followers interested in local farms and the farm to table movement. Building a Twitter following takes time and patience but is worth the time invested.

The best followers are the people who actively seek out small farms as future customers. The second-best way to gain followers is by advertising on Twitter. Twitter allows you to select your advertising audience based on geographic location and interests.

Step 3: Start Tweeting. Here are the five types of tweets.
1. **Tweet**: This is a straightforward message from you to your audience and is the most basic and straightforward tweet. This is the tweet that will promote farm products, services, or make announcements.

2. **@Reply**: This is a message sent as a reply to a received message. The @reply is a public message that mentions the Twitter username of the person, and it appears in the tweet stream of everyone who follows both profiles.
3. **Mention:** This is a message that references another Twitter username. It is always a good practice to have your farm name mentioned in as many tweets as possible, and mentioning other people is a great way to get people to mention you.
4. **Direct message (DM):** This a message sent privately to another Twitter user. You can only send a DM to someone who follows you. This is an excellent customer service or sales technique.
5. **Retweet (RT):** A message created and sent by someone else that you forward to your followers. Twitter makes this simple and easy.

Best Practices for Small Farms: Twitter

Best Practice 1: Tweet Content. For promotional purposes, you want to focus on brand messaging. Give people useful information, tips on how to store, cook, or use farm products and respond to customer questions.

Tweets do not need to be well-constructed or complex sentences. In the world of Twitter, sentence fragments and abbreviations are the norm. To develop your style, experiment, and use various ways to communicate the same message. Twitter's brevity requires focus and intentional word choice for a compelling message.

Best Practice 2: Increase Web Visitors. Tweets are electronic versions of headlines and classified ads. It is not always going to be possible to share all the information in a single tweet. Using tweets as an invitation to visit a farm's website for more detailed information is a great practice.

Best Practice 3: Interact with other Social Media. Twitter is a great source to let readers know that a new blog post is ready or new products are in your Facebook store. Use Twitter to make announcements when you do something meaningful on other social media sites.

Best Practice 4: Organize Twitter Lists. As you follow more people, it can be challenging to focus on the information coming from specific people and groups. To manage this, use Twitter lists. Twitter lists allow for the creation of different groups. For example, you may create separate lists for the following groups:

- Customers
- Potential customers
- Neighborhood or community businesses
- Trade or professional organizations
- Farm to table restaurants or retail stores
- Area farmers markets
- People who inspire you
- People you talk with the most

A list allows you to see the tweets from the list members as a separate Twitter timeline. This will enable you to keep track of what these people have or want to say. You can organize your lists in any way that helps you. This organization can include one or many lists, and it allows these lists to be public or private.

Conclusion

Twitter is popular. It is excellent for marketing and communication. This platform keeps you connected with current customers and puts you in contact with future customers. Twitter is simple and easy to use, but it needs proper management for maximum effectiveness.

Small Farm Internet Marketing Strategy 8: Facebook

*"Facebook was not originally created to be a company. It was built to accomplish a social mission - to make the world more open and connected." ~ **Mark Zuckerberg***

Facebook is the largest social networking site in the world. Facebook claims to have over 2 billion users! If you pick just one social media platform for marketing your farm, it should be Facebook.

Facebook is easy to use. It has excellent tools for small farms who direct market their products. For farmers who are data-driven, Facebook is perfect. It has data analysis tools that allow for the targeting of advertising by location, interests, likes, etc.

For small farms, homesteads, and market gardeners, Facebook is perfect. By creating a page for your farm, you are connecting people and building relationships. This page is an excellent source of information about your products, services, and events.

Four Steps to Using Facebook

Step 1: Profile Creation. To set up a profile, you will need a phone number or email address.
Step 2: Profile Verification. Facebook will use your email or phone number to verify you are a real person.

Step 3: Find Friends. Facebook will pull contact suggestions from your email or cell phone to make suggestions. Facebook allows you to search for friends by name.

Step 4: Advertise. This can be paid or free. Paid advertising requires setting up a business page, which is easy and painless. Free advertising requires finding people to like your farm's page, joining groups, and using Facebook Marketplace.

Eight Steps to Facebook Advertising

Step 1: Objective. Using your farm's profile, log in to Facebook Ads Manager. Select the Campaigns tab, and then click "create." This will start your Facebook marketing. Currently, Facebook offers 11 marketing objectives; pick the objective that most closely relates to your marketing goal.

Step 2: Campaign Name. Facebook allows you to set up what they call an A/B split test. This allows for easy monitoring of different ad versions. Use the objective name in the campaign name. For example, if you are selling a product, name the campaign after the product.

Step 3: Ad Account Creation. Facebook requires advertising accounts to have a debit or credit card linked to it. Also, the account requires that you pick your country, preferred currency, and time zone. Changing this information requires a new account.

Step 4: Audience Targeting. This is the most critical step, and the step most people get wrong. The biggest mistake is people select people who are like farmers when they need to target farm customers. As you build the target audience, focus on the type of person who buys from a farmers market and not the person selling at the farmers market.

Facebook allows you to narrow your target market to include or exclude people based on demographics, interests, and behaviors. For example, when marketing beef, I exclude vegans, vegetarians, and members of PETA, but include people who like grilling, steaks, and locally grown food.

Step 5: Connections: Facebook allows you to target or exclude people who have an existing connection to your Facebook Page, your app, or an event you promoted on Facebook. If the goal is for new likes from people who fit your customer's profile, you will select "exclude people who like your page."

If you want to promote a product or a special offer to your followers, select "People who like your Facebook Page" or "People who like your Facebook Page and their friends" to reach people who already know about your farm and their friends.

Step 6. Determine Ad Placements. Facebook will automatically place your ads across Facebook, Instagram, Messenger, and Audience Network, according to Facebook's algorithms. These algorithms place advertisements in the following areas:
- Device type: Mobile, desktop, or both.

- Platform: Facebook, Instagram, Audience Network, or Messenger, with several sub-options.
- Mobile devices and operating systems: iOS, Android, or both.

Step 7: Budget and Schedule. Facebook will gladly take all your money; therefore, be careful as you set your budget. Facebook allows advertisers to choose a daily or lifetime budget. Facebook marketing campaigns can start immediately or in any future period.

Step 8: Ad Creation. Select your ad format, and then enter the text and media components for it. The campaign objective determines available formats. When creating a Facebook ad, remember the following:

- Focus
- Readable font
- Minimal text
- Simplicity
- Call to action
- Professional videos, images, and graphics

Best Practices for Small Farms: Facebook

Best Practice 1. Facebook Groups. A Facebook group is an excellent place for people to get together and share information and ideas with like-minded users in an online community environment. There are two ways to get involved with groups – either create your own group or join an existing group.

Creating your own Facebook Group can be an effective way to gather your fans in one place and encourage them to interact with one another. Building an active community of people talking about your business is a great way to gather customer intelligence.

Join the right groups. The right groups will get your page more likes while connecting with people who want to buy farm products. Many communities have yard sale pages that allow people to buy and sell products. These groups are always a great place to post items for sale.

Best Practice 2. Monitor, Measure, and Mend. These three M's build audience engagement. Monitor what worked, what did not, and what you can do to improve. Measure the results and mend things as needed. The data from Facebook Insights can help you monitor, measure, and mend and ensure that advertising dollars are an investment and not an expense.

Best Practice 3: Geographic Targeting. A narrow geographic area may get fewer page likes, but this proximity can lead to more actual customers. For a small farm, the goal of Facebook is not to have the most likes but to gain customers.

Best Practice 4: Select the Right Interests. This is like trying to impress someone in a conversation. The absolute best way to start a conservation is to talk about the other person's interests. The same concept holds true for finding Facebook followers. The absolute best followers for a farm's Facebook page are the people who are going to purchase farm products, and attracting these people requires shared interests.

Best Practice 5: Proper Messaging. The right message requires continuously and consistently promoting a farm's brand story. Use intentionality when communicating with people via Facebook. When creating a message, careful consideration always produces the best results.

Best Practice 6: Earn Badges. Facebook offers badges for business profiles. Earning badges provides credibility with many of Facebook's most loyal users. The most critical badge for a farm is the verified badge, which confirms you are a business.

Best Practice 7: Get Reviews. Happy customers create great reviews. Positive reviews on a Farm's page increases the likelihood of new likes and selling products to new customers. If someone is not happy with a purchase, treat this as an opportunity to fix the problem and restore the relationship so that they will want to leave a positive review.

Best Practice 8: Wall Management. The wall is where the most personal action takes place on Facebook. This is where people make comments, ask questions, or post pictures. Managing this space is vital for a farm's Facebook reputation. Facebook allows you to monitor this area with various settings, and the most important of these is content approval.

Always approve what people are writing on your farm's page. Also, delete any negative posts or comments. This is your place on Facebook, and make sure this page truly reflects your farm's mission, values, and practices.

My wife taught me the importance of just deleting negative wall messages. I used to argue and engage these people. My wife pointed out that I was not changing their minds, they were not customers, and it just makes more sense to delete and block instead of engaging and encouraging. She was right.

Best Practice 9: Marketplace. Facebook marketplace is an online yard sale. Basically, people post items for sale in this forum. There are some limitations to Marketplace. For example, you cannot sell live animals, pets, or guns. If you violate these terms, Facebook will delete your post and send you a message. Repeated violations will get you banned from Marketplace.

Best Practice 10: Create a Store. Facebook allows you to create a store to sell products. This is a free service, and you should take advantage of it. Facebook stores come with the option to accept credit cards.

Best Practice 11: Follower Management. There is not a limit to the number of followers you can have on Facebook. Therefore, it may not hurt to have random people who never buy from you follow your page. Be sure to monitor this closely; you don't want a casual visitor to post inaccurate information. It is unlikely, but it is something to watch closely. When in doubt, block people from your farm's page. Remember – you control the messaging!

Conclusion

Your farm should be on Facebook. It is the most popular social media platform in the world. Customers expect businesses, including small farms, to be on Facebook. This is a great medium to share what is in season, hours, and upcoming events, along with other relevant information.

Small Farm Internet Marketing Strategy 9: Instagram

*"It helps to see the world through a different lens, and that's what we wanted to do with Instagram. We wanted to give everyone the same feeling of discovering the world around you through a different lens." ~ **Kevin Systrom***

Instagram is a photo and video-sharing social media platform owned by Facebook. Instagram's primary content is pictures and videos posted by community members. By design, Instagram makes it easy to share content across mobile devices.

Currently, Instagram has 800 million users, many of whom access the site many times a day. While Facebook may have the most users, Instagram has the most loyal users. This loyalty is an attractive feature for marketing and advertising purposes.

Instagram is a great online source to advertise a small farm. People like pictures of barns, animals, flowers, plants, and nature. (All easy to come by on a farm!) Instagram advertising is easy; all you need is a Facebook account and a business profile for your farm. To get started, here are four Instagram ads that are great for small farms:

1. **Photo Ads.** Photo ads allow you to tell your farm story and brand through images. Instagram photo ads put farm pictures in front of more people who may become customers.

2. **Video Ads.** Instagram users love videos. Video ads are great for highlighting a small farm in action. The best videos are funny, informative, and short. The most effective videos are under 30 seconds.

3. **Carousel Ads**. These ads allow users to swipe through a series of images or videos. These ads come with a call-to-action button allowing easy access to your farm's website. The multiple pictures in these ads allow greater opportunities to develop a longer brand story or to feature various products.

4. **Story Ads.** Instagram Story Ads are full-screen ads, which appear as a story or standard post. Stories expire after 24 hours, so this type of add is perfect for limited-time offers or promotions.

Best Practices for Small Farms: Instagram

Best Practice 1: Brand Alignment. Instagram is an excellent tool for keeping a farm's brand story alive and active. Instagram users immerse themselves in the platform, making the audience receptive to learning more about your brand's story, mission, values, and practices.

Best Practice 2: Regularity. Post daily or every other day. Starting out, weekly posts would be adequate, but Instagram works best if your posts are daily. If you visit multiple farmers markets, announce it the day before and on market day to let people know you are ready for business. Also, post pictures and videos of your animals, wildlife, or other farm happenings.

Best Practice 3: Understand the Audience. Do not forget who you are trying to reach. Customers are real people who are more than a set of demographics and interests. Instagram is a highly personal form of social media; therefore, be personal. This allows people to get personal with you.

Best Practice 4: Precise Phrasing. An image is worth a thousand words! Therefore, let the pictures do the talking and not the words. Keep your text and captions brief unless you have something meaningful to say.

Intentionally develop your caption text with a focus on your audience's interests. Write effective call-to-action statements that compel people to click on your ad, visit your website, make a purchase, or like your profile. Hashtags are an essential part of Instagram and can increase your reach and relevance.

Best Practice 5: Consistency. According to Instagram, sixty percent of the top brands on Instagram use the same filter for every post. Consistency builds brand recognition. Each ad element needs to represent who you are as a small farm.

Best Practice 6: Stay Fresh. Instagram ads are like produce; they have a limited shelf life. Some high performing ads may have the staying power of winter squash while some are more like a tomato. The best ads will fade and lose effectiveness. Keeping ads fresh keeps people engaged.

Best Practice 7: Experiment. Experiment and keep track of which audiences, ads, text, pictures, and videos work best for your farm.

Best Practice 8: Hashtags. Hashtags are vital when posting on Instagram. Hashtags have their own section, and you may want to review that section. Instagram hashtags boost engagement by 12.6 percent on average. Use hashtags relevant to your audience and popular with the farm to table movement. Make sure your farm's name is its own hashtag and tag every post with #yourfarmname.

Conclusion

Instagram allows you to share pictures with customers in a way that can increase customer engagement. Instagram is a great way to share your farm's story visually in real-time. It is also a great place to let your farm's personality come through. The reality of a working farm will be engaging for most followers.

Small Farm Internet Marketing Strategy 10: YouTube

"The joy of YouTube is that you can create content about anything you feel passionate about, however silly the subject matter." ~ ***Zoe Sugg***

YouTube, a Google company, is the world's most popular video-sharing platform. YouTube consistently rates in the top five most popular social media platforms and is the second most popular search platform (not engine) next to Google.

YouTube is more popular than cable TV, and that popularity soars with 18–48 year-olds who consume YouTube at twice the rate of cable! For small farmers, this provides an advertising opportunity that connects marketing messages with people actively searching for farm-related products.

Advertising with ads on YouTube requires a Google AdSense account. If you do not have a Google account, you will need to set one up. If you have a Google account or a Google Business account, this first step is complete.

Google has a video tutorial to walk people through the advertising process. This video does a much better job of explaining the process than I can in this book; more importantly, the video is current with Google's updates. Google advertising is easy; there is no need to pay anyone for this.

AdSense on YouTube allows high-level customization and targeting. This targets geographic areas, specific groups based on particular attributes, distinctive behaviors, and traditional demographics. (There is a discussion about this in the Google Section.)

A YouTube channel is a valuable marketing channel, as well as a vibrant brand-building tool. The YouTube channel is the control center of the YouTube experience, showing a person's history, video likes, video subscriptions, and uploaded videos.

The absolute best thing about creating videos is content control. Developing and uploading videos allows you to express who you are, what you do, and why you do it - all on your own terms.

Originality, innovation, and creativity are the driving forces of businesses that grow and become sustainable. Creating videos taps into those forces. Besides, television or video advertising, historically, is the most effective form of advertising; YouTube has made that medium accessible to anyone with a smartphone or webcam.

Whether using Google AdSense or developing videos, follow these ten best practices.

Best Practices for Small Farms: YouTube

Best Practice 1: Brand Awareness. YouTube makes it easy to share farm practices, farm products, farm life, and for people to get to know you as a farmer.

Best Practice 2: Plan. Before recording, clarify your purpose, think through what you will say, decide who will say what, and choose a location.

Best Practice 3: Plan Execution. Record the video with as many takes as needed. Recording a video is like anything else on the farm - it never goes the way you plan. Animals and the weather will not cooperate but keep recording until you get a solid rough draft with ample content.

Best Practice 4: Video Editing. Most smartphones or computers come with video editing software. For a more professional, polished look, use one of the many different professional software options available. This process can be extremely simple or amazingly complex. For a small farm, it makes more sense for this to be simple. This makes the farm approachable, real, and authentic.

Best Practice 5: Announcements. This can be a product launch, new building, baby animals, event, or something else. YouTube is a great way to build anticipation about future happenings, products, and events.

Best Practice 6: Native Content. The most effective small farm promotional videos feature the farm in its most natural state. Most of your videos need to be farm-based with an occasional video from a farmers market or roadside stand.

Best Practice 7: Product Demonstrations. Create cooking, canning, preserving, or other how-to videos. Provide people examples and guides on how to use and to get the most from your farm products.

Best Practice 8: Stay Simple. There is no need to complicate things. Keep videos short, simple, and salient. Most people watching videos on YouTube are not looking for a full-length show; they are looking for something quick and easy to watch. How-to videos are a natural tie-in for a small farm. How do you know if a watermelon is ripe, or how do you make a fence from pallets? Your YouTube channel could answer these questions. Staying simple, focused, and direct will attract new watchers for your content.

Best Practice 9: Website and Social Media Promotion. This allows people to learn more about your farm while enabling them to connect with you. The goal is to turn subscribers into customers.

Best Practice 10: Fun. Producing, editing, and sharing your farm must be fun. Farming is fun and making videos shares that fun with the world. The easiest way to do this is to share your joy of farming with the world.

Conclusion

YouTube captures the live action of a small farm. Video advertising has always been the most effective form of advertising. Developing a YouTube channel, creating videos, and sharing your farm journey creates personal connections with current and future customers.

Appendix

The following are marketing items that are important for small farm marketing but did not fit elsewhere in the book.

Quick Response Codes (QR Codes)

These codes are a type of barcode with a matrix of black and white scribbly dots. These dots provide product information to users with a QR scanner or app. When people scan this code, they get additional product information through a link to your farm's website (or social medial).

A QR code can also be used to place orders, get discounts, subscribe to a mailing list, or just about anything else you can imagine. A QR code brings farm marketing into the modern era while providing a farm with five benefits:
1. **Market Integration.** A QR code connects print and online advertising. People are likely to toss away print material; however, QR codes encourage scanning. When people scan this code to find a farm's website or social media, they are more likely to connect with that farm when they are ready to purchase.
2. **Social media followers**. By having a QR code on display at a roadside stand or farmers market booth, it is easy for customers to find and follow a farm's social media.
3. **Measurable.** QR codes make tracking market efforts easier. This allows you to see what advertising is working, what needs adjusting, and what needs elimination.

4. **Novelty.** Producers in the farm to table movement are often behind the times. When using a QR code, you are standing out from other farmers while creating an exciting way for people to engage with your farm.
5. **Inexpensive.** QR codes are cheap and many times free thanks to online tools that generate a simple code for you to download.

154 Farm phrases, Taglines, and Slogans

Having a phrase, tagline, or slogan is essential. The word slogan comes from the Gaelic word "slaugh-ghairm," meaning, "war cry." The marketplace is brutal, so the evolutionary development of this word makes sense. Throughout history, conquerors used war cries to strike fear into opponents as well as to rally the troops. A slogan, tagline, or farm-marketing phrase should do the same.

A slogan must summarize a brand in just a few words. Effective slogans have three components. First, they must be likable. Test likability by asking customers, friends, family, and employees their opinions. Second, slogans connect with feelings. People need to have an emotional attachment to the slogan. Lastly, they must be concise. People will never remember a slogan that is wordy, rambling, or tedious.

Here is a list of farm-related slogans. A few are original, but most of them are commonly used or obvious slogans. The goal of this list is to help you develop a unique slogan, and not for you to just pick a slogan to use.

Slogan	Comment
All nature (natural)	
All nature (natural) all the time	
Amazing meat	
As nature intended	
Awesome meat	
Awesome produce	
Barn approved	
Beef it up	
Better than organic	

Beyond organic	
Chemical free produce	
Child approved	
Crafted with love	
Customer approved	
Customer certified organic	
Dirt raised	
Family approved	
Family farm raised	
Farm products for a better world	
Farm products for healthy living	
Farm products that taste right	
Farmer approved	
Farmer approved family loved	
Feed your family for life	
Feed your family right	
Feeding you like family	
Feeding your family like ours	
Filler free meat	
Filler free produce	
Food that tastes like food	
Food that won't kill you	
Forested pork	
Free range chicken	
Full flavor produce	
Good food is our obsession	
Good food is our passion	
Growing quality	
Grown with love	
Hand crafted	
Hand fed cattle	
Hand fed chickens	
Hand gathered	
Hand grown	
Hand nurtured	
Hand raised	
Happy chickens make better eggs	
Happy chickens make better	

meat	
Happy cows make better meat	
Happy cows make better milk	
Harvesting plenty	
Harvesting quality	
Harvesting the best for you	
Harvesting the best for your family	
Healthy food for healthy living	
Herbicide free produce	
Hippy grown	
Hippy inspired	
Hippy loved	
If bugs won't eat it why should you	
Imperfect produce that is perfectly good	
Imperfectly perfect produce	
Inspired by nature	
Know your farmer	
Leader in the field	
Life changing meat	
Life-changing produce	
Local flavor	
Local harvest	
Locally connected	
Locally grown	
Locally raised	
Locally sourced	
Mother Nature approved	
Mother nature is our partner	
Natural processes	
Natural processes	
Naturally grown	
Naturally raised	
Naturally raised for naturally good taste	
Nature approved	
Nature raised and loved	

Nonfactory farm egg	
Nonfactory farm beef	
Nonfactory farm chicken	
Noncertified organic	
Not government approved	
Nothing replaces nature	
Nurtured with love	
Open range chicken	
Organically inspired	
Our chickens live outside	
Our food our passion	
Our harvest your food	
Our produce our passion	
Partnered with nature	
Pasture chicken	
Pasture perfect	
Pasture-raised	
Pasture-raised chicken	
Pastured pork	
Pasture-raised meat	
Pesticide-free produce	
Poly grass-fed	
Produce for a changing world	
Produce that saves lives	
Rain watered, dirt grown	
Raised outdoors	
Real food for real people	
Real food nothing added	
Real food tastes like this	
Real food is healthy	
Safe food for your family	
Salad bar beef	
Saving the planet one harvest at a time	
Saving the world one harvest at the time	
Say no to industrial farming	
Share in our bounty	
Share in our harvest	

Sharing our best	
Small farms do it better	
Small farm over factory farm	
Small farm-raised	
Small farming is a way of life	
Small farms are better	
Small farms care	
Small farms provide food security	
Small farms saving the environment	
Small farms the backbone of America	
Soiled based produce	
Sun and dirt are our secret ingredients	
Support local agriculture	
Support small farms	
Support your local farmer	
Sustainable food for sustainable living	
Taste of fresh	
Taste of home	
Water added while growing not during packing	
We eat our meat	
We get our hands dirty, so you don't have to	
We love our animals so you will too	
We were raised in a barn	
We work with nature	
What we feed our kids	
What we feed ourselves	
Where does your food come from?	

Words to Describe Farms

Here is a list of words to use when describing your farm.

Agrarian
Artisan
Cage-free
Chemical-free
Clean
Community
Cultivate
Craft
Environmental
Ethical
Family
Farm to Table
Free Range
Fresh
Grass-fed
Healing
Healthier
Heirloom
Heritage

Holistic
Husbandry
Legacy
Local
Natural
Non-GMO
Pasture
Polyculture
Regenerative
Rejuvenate
Restorative farming
Salad bar
Self-sustaining
Soil
Sustainable
Technique
Trade
Tradition
Traditionally Raised

Words or Phrases to Describe Competition

Here is a list of words to describe the competition as defined as big box stores, large retailers, and other large companies, organizations, and corporations. These words do not represent other small farmers down the road or other vendors at farmers markets.

Big-Ag
Big box
Big food
Bio-engineered
Chemical
Conventionally raised
Corporate
Corporate farm
Death by data
Dumbed down products
Exploitation
Faceless
Factory Farm
Feedlot
Fillers
GMO

Greedy
Homogeneous
Industrial AG
Manipulative
Mass-produced
Money driven
Monoculture
Profit-driven not quality driven
Profits over environment
Scientifically designed
Suicide seeds
Small farm killer
Small town killer
Standardization

Quotes

In writing and researching this book, I collected many quotes useful for small farmers who have big ideas, big plans, and big dreams. Many quotes found their way into various pages of this book as well as in chapter headers. Here are some extras that didn't make it in.

I share these quotes with the hopes that you find them insightful, useful, and inspirational. I offer no explanation or reason for these quotes so that you will develop your own interpretation and use. It is my desire that this book helps you to become original, live your dreams, and grow your own way.

"The world as we have created it is a process of our thinking. It cannot be changed without changing our thinking."
~Albert Einstein

"Without ambition one starts nothing. Without work one finishes nothing. The prize will not be sent to you. You have to win it." ~ **Ralph Waldo Emerson**

"Leaders are limited by their vision rather than by their abilities." ~ **Roy T. Bennett**

"An artist is not paid for his labor but for his vision." ~ **James Whistler**

"You don't learn to walk by following rules. You learn by doing and falling over." ~ **Richard Branson**

"The way to get started is to quit talking and begin doing."
~**Walt Disney**

"An entrepreneur tends to bite off a little more than he can chew hoping he'll quickly learn how to chew it." ~ **Roy Ash**

"Don't dwell on what went wrong. Instead, focus on what to do next. Spend your energies on moving forward toward finding the answer." ~ **Denis Waitley**

"Marketing is not bragging, and touting one's wares is not evil. The baker in the medieval town square must holler, 'Fresh rolls!' if he hopes to feed the townfolk." ~ **Jeffrey Zeldman**

"Whatever the mind can conceive and believe, it can achieve."
~**Napoleon Hill**

"Go confidently in the direction of your dreams. Live the life you have imagined." ~ **Henry David Thoreau**

"The thinking that guides your intelligence is much more important than how much intelligence you have."
~ **David Schwartz**

"The mind is a fertile land and the crop depends on what you sow and how you nurture." ~ **Myra Yadav**

"Ignore others, forget about the competition, and focus on living your dreams and grow your own way." ~*Jason McClure*

Also available on Amazon

This book is on a mission to save the planet. According to Yale Environment 360, "Human activities are causing an alarming decline in biodiversity that is endangering food security, clean water, energy supplies, economies, and livelihoods." Raising and marketing heirloom vegetables provides a viable solution to that problem. This book makes the case that heirlooms are vital to the planet and that heirlooms can increase a small farm's profitability.

This book details 15 reasons why heirlooms are superior to modern scientifically engineered vegetables, how to brand heirloom produce, and 22 proven heirloom marketing tips. Also, it offers marketing information, descriptions, and tips for 473 different heirloom varieties. For each heirloom profiled, this book describes its history, competitive advantage, marketing tips, sales strategies, production, companion planting, uses, and fun facts.

This book is an information-packed marketing guide that will help farmers sell more produce to more people while doing something great for the planet. This incredible resource belongs in the library of all mission-driven farms and garden enthusiasts. "This book provides the tools to grow heirlooms in the garden as well as in the market. It is a map for restoring heirloom produce to mainstream production and returning family farms to profitability.

The essential leadership guide for small farms, market gardeners, and homesteaders. Farms are the pursuit of a noble ideal based on purpose, passion, and pride. These three Ps are something all visionary, authentic, and inspirational leaders have in common.

'Finally, a REAL leadership for real farmers.'

Jason McClure

SMALL FARM
LEADERSHIP

AN INSIDE
OUT APPROACH FOR GROWING FARMS,
PEOPLE, AND PROFITS

A GROW YOUR OWN WAY PUBLICATION

Small Farm Leadership
An inside out approach for growing farms, people, and profits.

Many people want to be in charge, make decisions, and to be in control. Fewer people understand what it takes to be effective in a position of power, whether that position of power is formal or informal.

This book teaches what it takes to be a small farm leader. It is an inside-outside approach to leadership, and unlike other leadership books, this book focuses on the needs of small farms, homesteads, urban gardens, and rural America.

This book is different from farm management books, which focuses on operations, tasks, and manipulation methods; this book focuses on how to create visionary leadership and how to thrive in what many people consider a declining industry.

Written in an easy to digest format, this book is packed with information, insights, and strategies. This book is not another farm memoir written by a farm aristocrat. It is a guidebook written by someone who believes small farms are economic engines that can provide a great living to their owners, and opportunity still exists in rural America.

www.ingramcontent.com/pod-product-compliance
Lightning Source LLC
Chambersburg PA
CBHW021351210526
45463CB00001B/62